A Recipe to Market Your Book

21 Steps to Book Marketing Success!

M. Carroll

What's inside this book?

A note from Anamcara Press iv
   Congratulations! iv
Introduction to Marketing v
   Develop Your Marketing Plan v
   What You'll Find in This Book vii
1. Marketing Plan Timeline 1
   21 Step Timeline & Checklist for Marketing Your Book 1
2. Marketing Plan Outline 7
   Abbreviated 21 Step Timeline for Marketing Your Book 7
3. Marketing Plan Narrative 9
   Create a marketing Narrative from your 21 Step Timeline 9
4. Marketing Plan Worksheet 13
   Your Book Marketing Plan Assignments 13
   Section I: Seven Assignments 14
   Section Ii: Marketing Plan Worksheet 19
   Section Iii: Putting It All Together 22
   Marketing Questionnaire 24
   Map Your Route! 25
   Marketing Activities Worksheet 26
   Write A Media Pitch 28
   Beware of Scams! 31
5. Ebook Focused Strategy 33
   Tried And True Ebook Strategies To Review 33
   Ebook Discounted Promotion Websites 39
6. Online Marketing Plan of Action 41
   Next Steps: Creating Good Marketing Habits 41
   Social Media Marketing Steps 42
   Email Marketing Steps 44
   Website Marketing 46
   Blogging Steps 46
7. YouTube Marketing 48
   3 YouTube Strategies to Adopt 48

8. Paid Online Advertising 50
Facebook, Amazon, Online Rags 50
Facebook Advertising Steps 51
Amazon Advertising Steps 52

9. Paid Print Advertising 54
Is Print Advertising Dead? 54
Sample Print Ad 55

10. Direct Sales 56
Sell Yourself and Your Book Directly 56
Direct Sales Steps 56

Count Down! 64
Prepare for your book's launch 64
Launch Steps 64

Resources 65
Follow up on your marketing knowledge 65

Authors are Awesome! 66
Thank you for being an author! 66

Recipes

1. Check list Party Mix 6
2. Marketing Mozzarella Salad 11
3. Worksheet Gluten-free Sheet Cake 32
4. Co-Author Cherry Upside-Down Cake 40
5. NetGalley Spicy Navy & Spinach Bean Soup 47
6. EBook Deviled Eggs 49
7. Headway Hummus 53
8. Pre-Launch Chilli Pie 57

You can market alone, or you can work together (perhaps remotely) and share ideas and recipes with fellow authors!

a note from Anamcara Press LLC

IN THE COMPANY OF BOOKS

~ OUR FRIENDS

Anamcara Press publishes select works and brings writers & artists together in collaborations that serve community and the planet.

Maureen (Micki) Carroll

M. Carroll is a writer, educator, photographer and graphic designer. She founded Anamcara Press in 2014 with the mission of publishing select works and bringing writers & artists together in collaborations that serve community and the planet.

Carroll has published several books, "The Tree Who Walked Through Time ~ A Tree Identification Story," "A Wyoming Cowboy in Hitler's Germany," "Spiders Dance," "The Raspberry Race," and "Consciousness: An Owner's Manual." Carroll has also published many non-fiction articles & training programs, and blogs about consciousness and community at maureencarroll.com.

CONGRATULATIONS!

You've completed a book! That is a major accomplishment, one that many dream of but few achieve. Now it's time to get to work!

Marketing your book is a very different activity from writing. When writing you mostly use your right brain—the hemisphere that is visual and intuitive. Although both hemispheres work together to perform cognitive tasks, it is generally thought that the left hemisphere processes information in a more verbal, analytical manner—better for marketing—while the right part of the brain is more non-verbal & creative.

I personally find writing & marketing to be mutually exclusive because they each require something different from me. Most authors have trouble doing marketing activities comfortably.

However, just as it is necessary to set time aside to write and get those creative juices flowing, it is also necessary to set time aside to promote your book. The goal of this guide is to help you sharpen up your left-hemisphere and get started marketing!

He who hesitates is lost.
But he who seems lost may simply be wandering.

MARKET YOUR BOOK!
HTTPS://ANAMCARA-PRESS.COM/

Introduction to Marketing

This guide was created for authors as part of our commitment to you and your writing!

Anamcara Press is a small independent publisher that releases fewer than ten select works each year. As a boutique press, we partner with authors to help them achieve their vision and find their audience.

Anamcara Press seeks to publish powerful voices that serve community and the planet. While we publish only a few authors per year, we do offer publishing assistance to independent authors and produce books, articles, blogs, and videos to assist authors everywhere. Whether you are an author or an artist, or both, you need a marketing plan.

Develop Your Marketing Plan

A marketing plan is your blueprint for success. It will guide your book promotion activities. It is also required in order to gain acceptance by the big four bookstores: Costco, Booksamillion, Hudson News, and Barnes & Noble.

These humongous booksellers require sales of 500+ books, an established author platform, and a detailed marketing plan for consideration. This book aims to help you achieve this lofty goal by helping you:

- Establish your author platform
- Create a competitive marketing plan for your book's promotion
- Implement your marketing plan to achieve 500+ sales and entry to a wider audience

Marketing is no longer about the stuff that you make, but about the stories you tell.

— Seth Godin

Opportunity is missed by most people because it is dressed in overalls and looks like work.

— Thomas Edison

MARKET YOUR BOOK!
HTTPS://ANAMCARA-PRESS.COM/

Marketing Guidance in 10 Chapters
What You'll Find in This Book

To help you create effective actions and language for your book marketing plan, this book includes: a 21 step marketing timeline, a marketing plan outline, a marketing plan sample narrative, and a marketing plan worksheet. There are detailed marketing strategies in chapters 5-10, and in the appendix a comprehensive list of resources including: bookstores, libraries, NPR stations, bloggers, reviewers, and more. *You'll also find delicious recipes to share with your marketing team!*

Chapter 1
A Book Marketing Plan Timeline provides a detailed 21 step guide for marketing your book.

Chapter 2
A Book Marketing Plan Outline, you'll find a summary of your 21 step timeline in outline form to help you stay organized.

Chapter 3
A Book Marketing Plan Narrative, you'll find a sample timeline narrative to customize for your marketing plan narrative. This is part one of your plan.

Chapter 4
A Book Marketing Plan Worksheet, you'll find a 7 step guide for writing part two of your marketing plan narrative.

Chapter 5
Ebook Focused Strategy, provides a summary of online focused efforts for your eBook.

Chapter 6
Online Marketing Strategy provides a summary of online focused efforts for your print and eBook.

Chapter 7
YouTube Marketing Strategy provides a summary of YouTube focused efforts for your print and eBook.

Chapter 8
Paid Online Advertising Strategy provides a summary of paid online advertising opportunities through Facebook and Amazon

Chapter 9
Paid Print Advertising Strategy provides a summary of print advertising options for your print and eBook.

Chapter 10
Direct Sales Strategy offers guidance on contacting bookstores, libraries, and media for your print and eBook.

Marketing Plan Timeline

Follow these best practices to help your book succeed. Digest it slowly and take it step-by-step!

21 Step Timeline & Checklist for Marketing Your Book

PART ONE: PREPARE BOOK

1. **EDIT & DESIGN**—Professional proofread, layout & typographical design of interior & cover
   - [ ] Select Title (Subtitle)
   - [ ] Determine Book Size & Format (Hard/Soft/Ebook)
   - [ ] Photography And Photo Preparation (If Needed)
   - [ ] Select Interior Chapter Layout And Typographical Design
   - [ ] Select Cover Design
   - [ ] Branding

2. **WRITE METADATA**—Establish keywords & descriptive language (author bio/book hook)
   - [ ] BLURBS: create 4000 character blurb about the book and author; a short description of 350 words; an even shorter description of 350 characters; and a twitter post of 280 characters or less
   - [ ] IDENTIFIERS: select three categories to identify book; BISAC Category (Book Industry Standards & Communications category) based on your book's genre; include regions, Author/contributor bio, previous work and publications, affiliations
   - [ ] KEY WORDS: Google Keyword Planner - adwords account—tools & analytics; https://adwords.google.com/KeywordPlanner—click search for new keyword & adgroup ideas; (also title search 10000-100,000); Go to the "Distribute" tab. Click on the description link and scroll down until you see the search keyword box.
   - [ ] PRICE: determine pricing for all three versions before first upload (cost of book wholesale/retail with 55% discount.)
   - [ ] RELEASE DATES: select release date (complete book & begin marketing 6+ months earlier)

Media Kit Includes:

Reviews & Awards

Publisher Information

Title

Mock Up & Representative Graphic

Author & Illustrator Bio & Pics

Detailed Description

Isbn, Format, Price, Page Count, Copyright Year, Trim Size, Illustrations, Age Level (For Kids' Books), Genre

Table Of Contents And/Or Sample Text/Chapter

Website/Amazon Links

3. ASSIGN ISBN—Distributable ISBN numbers for each format
   - [ ] Soft
   - [ ] Hard
   - [ ] Ebook (Including Ebook, Kobe, Kindle, Etc.)
   - [ ] Audio Book
   - [ ] Other (Coloring Book, Puzzle, Etc.)

Your Book Is Now Ready For Upload For Distribution!

4. Order Proof Copies To Review
   - [ ] Review proof copies
   - [ ] Make needed changes
   - [ ] Second upload with changes

PART TWO: GATHER PRE-RELEASE REVIEWS OF BOOK

5. SEND ARCs (Advanced Reader Copies—not for sale) TO READERS
   - [ ] Prep PFD for Advanced Reader Copies (ARCs)
   - [ ] Send PDF or ARC to friends, informal readers/reviewers
   - [ ] Add selected reviews to book cover and/or interior (for readers who submit a review
   - [ ] Send an email request to review on amazon with link (see sample letters in appendix.)

6. PREPARE STAGE ONE MARKETING MATERIALS FROM METADATA
   - [ ] Review branding elements
   - [ ] Create media kit / press release
   - [ ] Create/update author website
   - [ ] Create/update author amazon page
   - [ ] Create/update author goodreads page
   - [ ] Create a signature at the bottom of your e-mails that points people to the url where they can purchase a copy of your book.
   - [ ] Create signatures that have the book url at the bottom of any message you post.

7. SEND BOOKS FOR EDITORIAL REVIEWS
   - [ ] Select editorial reviewers based on book genre
   - [ ] Order reviewer copies
   - [ ] Send to reviewers along with Stage One Marketing Materials

   (you'll find a list of reviewers in the appendix; always check details as people and addresses change!)

MARKET YOUR BOOK!
HTTPS://ANAMCARA-PRESS.COM/

WAIT 3-4 MONTHS FOR REVIEWS

8. PREPARE STAGE TWO MARKETING MATERIALS
   - [ ] Book release ad for print and web
   - [ ] Author/book business cards, 3 x 5 cards (or 4 x 6), and review request flyers
   - [ ] Book landing page (funnel to ecommerce and Amazon)
   - [ ] Book & author youtube videos
     - 30 seconds - 1 minute ad
     - 3-5 minute informational
     - 15-30 minute in-depth
     - Author Interview (also in writing to provide to media/bloggers as PDF)
   - [ ] create author-written articles (for print and E-media/bloggers/interviewers)

9. *ENGAGE MARKETING PRE-RELEASE PLAN*
   - [ ] plan email advertising campaign/link landing page
   - [ ] plan social media campaign (join and post regularly four or more):
     - Goodreads
     - YouTube
     - Facebook book/author page
     - LinkedIn announcements
     - Twitter
     - Instagram

10. UPDATE BOOK PRE-RELEASE (potentially after Receiving Reviews)
    - [ ] add Review blurbs and any final changes
    - [ ] create eBook and hard cover book from paperback
    - [ ] assign ISBN's to hard cover and eBook
    - [ ] pre-release book 2-3 months prior to publication date

MARKET YOUR BOOK!
HTTPS://ANAMCARA-PRESS.COM/

11. BEGIN MARKETING AND PROMOTION PRE-RELEASE

- [ ] Develop calendar of author events including release date of each version
- [ ] Create / share event ads for email and social media based on above events
- [ ] Ensure Amazon, Goodreads, Facebook author page activity by adding videos/articles (Share!! *You want to create some buzz before the release!*)
- [ ] Send author article/short writings with media kit to organizations/magazines/newspapers/blogs, regional booksellers, and national / international booksellers for book/author event consideration (you'll find a list of bookstores, etc. in the appendix, always check details as people and addresses change!)

12. SET UP AUTHOR EVENTS—Book signings at bookstores & libraries, print & online media interviews and blog interviews

- [ ] Event #1 = Release Event—This event helps determine the release date of the book!
- [ ] Event #2 = Private Party—Celebrate and reward friends and request Amazon/Goodreads reviews from those who have supported you (this event occurs shortly after or before release event—ensure folks come to public release, too!)
- [ ] Event at local library
- [ ] Event at local bookstore or other local venue
- [ ] Event at bookstores and libraries in cities where author has affiliations. Set up author book signing events / interviews concentrated during a 3-6 month window up to and after the release of book
- [ ] Set up on-line author events including blog interviews and Facebook live

PART THREE: RELEASE BOOK

13. ANNOUNCEMENT AND LAUNCH—Get the word out about your book's publication!

- [ ] Send notice of book's publication and related event(s) to media
- [ ] Send email notice about book's publication and related event(s) to all
- [ ] Share on-line ads to social media
- [ ] Distribute media kit containing information about book (with blurbs) far and wide
- [ ] Arrange a private party for your supporters and encourage attendees to bring their Kindles and Kobos and Nooks to the event so they can download the ebook there and then. Encourage attendees to write a review on amazon or goodreads within 7 days.

MARKET YOUR BOOK!
HTTPS://ANAMCARA-PRESS.COM/

14. LIBRARY & BOOKSTORE BOOK RELEASE EVENTS:
- [ ] arrange book signing(s) (advertise each event with press release, email notice, and social media ad)
- [ ] work with venue's marketing team to coordinate Social Media Advertising
- [ ] distribute mailchimp campaign
- [ ] distribute print book release ads for event promotion at pre-selected local venues
- [ ] Encourage attendees to write a review on Amazon or Goodreads within 7 days.
- [ ] take pictures and video and post on social media after the event

15. BOOK RELEASE ONLINE EVENT:
- [ ] arrange online event as guest blogger/podcast
- [ ] distribute ads for guest blogger event through social media
- [ ] Facebook "Live" presence for Q & A during specific times
- [ ] Goodreads/Amazon promotion

PART FOUR: POST RELEASE — *3 year marketing plan*

Consider the marketing story of *Elf on the Shelf*—today a phenomenon, but it had a very slow start. Their success came several years after the book launched. They kept marketing and were creative in their efforts. Have you adopted an Elf?

16. SEND BOOKS FOR AWARDS -
- [ ] select award organization based on book genre
- [ ] order & submit copies as determined by award guidelines (some charge.)
- [ ] Send along with Stage One Marketing Materials *(you'll find a list of award organizations in the appendix; always check details as things change!)*

17. CONTINUE TO ARRANGE SPEAKING ENGAGEMENTS & BOOK SIGNINGS
18. IF YOU HAVE A "NICHE MARKET," TARGET THAT MARKET (e.g., A book of poems with environmental emphasis would be pitched to environmental organizations, etc.)
19. PARTICIPATE IN BOOK FAIRS (SELL YOUR BOOKS FROM A BOOTH). *(You'll find a list of fairs & festivals in the appendix.)*
20. PARTICIPATE IN THE AMERICAN LIBRARY ASSOCIATION ANNUAL CONFERENCE
21. CARRY YOUR BOOK & BUSINESS CARD WITH YOU EVERYWHERE!

Recipe for Success!

A delicious recipe to share with your marketing team!
Feed your soul with good friends, feed your writing with good ideas, feed your stomach with good food.
Keep those creative juices flowing!

Check list Party Mix

Ingredients
6 cups Chex cerials
1 cup nuts of choice (almonds, cashews & pecans prefered!)
1 cup bite-sized pretzels
1 cup Cheerios
1 cup small Freetos
1 cup M&Ms
6 Tbsp worcestershire sauce
2 Tbsp of butter
1 tsp garlic powder (or more to taste)
1/2 tsp onion powder
1 1/2 tsp salt

Combine all dry ingredients except seasonings in a large bowl. Melt butter and add worcestershire sauce and seasonings. Drench dry ingredients with liquid. Slow cook at 225 for at least an hour on baking sheet stirring every 15 minutes. After baking and cooling, add M&Ms.
***Candy the pecans separately and add after, too.**

~ Cathy Martin
Illustrator: *The Tree Who Walked Through Time*
http://cathymartin4art.com/

MARKET YOUR BOOK!
HTTPS://ANAMCARA-PRESS.COM/

Marketing Plan Outline

An outline of your detailed 21 Step Timeline can be a useful tool for summarizing your intentions and reviewing your progress.

Abbreviated 21 Step Timeline for Marketing Your Book

PART ONE: PREPARE BOOK

1. Prepare soft cover print book, including editing, proof reading, professional layout & typographical design of interior and cover. (After preparing the soft cover, metadata is created & the book is then assigned an ISBN for each format.)

2. Prepare Metadata - detailed information about the author and book

3. Assign an ISBN for each format: soft cover, hard cover with jacket, ebook, and audio book

4. Order proof copies to review

PART TWO: GATHER PRE-RELEASE REVIEWS OF BOOK

5. Send ARCs to readers

6. Prepare stage one marketing materials including: media kit / press release; create/update author website; create/update author Amazon page; create/update author Goodreads page; create a signature at the bottom of author e-mails that points people to book sales page

7. Send book for editorial reviews

8. Prepare stage two marketing materials including: book release ad for print & web; author/book business cards & review request flyers; book landing page (funnel to AC Press e commerce & Amazon); book & author YouTube promotional videos;

9. Plan email advertising campaign (using combined contacts of publisher/author) & link landing page; and plan social media campaign.

10. Update Book Prior To Release. Add Review blurbs/Awards & any final changes

MARKET YOUR BOOK!
HTTPS://ANAMCARA-PRESS.COM/

11. Prepare Stage three marketing materials including: calendar of author events; event ads for email and social media; Amazon, Goodreads, Facebook author page presence; author article/short writings published in organizational newsletters/magazines/newspapers/blogs

12. Set up author events

PART THREE: RELEASE BOOK

13. Announcement & launch

14. Library/bookstore author signings

15. Online author release events

PART FOUR: POST-RELEASE—3 year strategy

16. Send published book for relevant awards in its genre

17. Arrange speaking engagements at book stores, special interest groups, or organizations

18. Find "niche market," target that market (e.g., a book of poems with environmental emphasis would be pitched to environmental organizations, etc.)

19. Participate in book fairs (sell your books from a booth). (find a list of fairs & festivals in the appendix)

20. Participate at the American Library Association annual conferences

21. Carry book & business card and distribute regularly

Marketing Plan Narrative

Customizable Sample Narrative

Create a marketing Narrative from your 21 Step Timeline

Customize the following timeline narrative to reflect your marketing activities to date, and what you plan to do in the future.

To Whom it May Concern:

The author has a 21 step marketing plan for BOOK by AUTHOR, (please see accompanying media kit.)

BOOK marketing plan includes the release of editions in soft cover, hard cover with jacket, ebook, and audio book. We have already accomplished successful book release events, and we continue to contact local & regional bookstores for interest in author events and stocking this engaging, LITERARY TRADE NOVEL.

In addition to designing each format of the book, the author developed a comprehensive marketing plan utilizing specific strategies and tactics.

The author has created and followed a timeline and calendar that addressed each

segment of the marketing plan. The author developed a pre-release strategy that focused on gaining editorial reviews and promoting the book for maximum exposure prior to publication.

The author developed a post-release strategy that focused on promoting the book to local, regional, and national bookstores and libraries; showing the book at the annual American Library Association Book Fair and other trade shows & book fairs; and submitting the book to appropriate book award opportunities throughout the year.

MARKET YOUR BOOK!
HTTPS://ANAMCARA-PRESS.COM/

We have identified the book's and author's target audience and branded both the author and the book accordingly, implementing the branding across all platforms and websites. We've also branded promotional materials prepared from carefully selected metadata, including a media kit/press release, and advertisements for social media and print.

We have established a social media platform to communicate effectively with and grow the book's target audience both pre and post-release.

In addition to the author's website, we've created a landing page for the book and YouTube videos shared by the author on their website, and posted on social media sites.

We also plan to make the book available to international publishers looking to purchase foreign language rights.

Sincerely,
Author

This narrative is only part one of your two part marketing plan narrative. Read and complete the following worksheet—what you write on the worksheet will become part two of your finished written marketing plan.

Jot down your ideas & have some fun with it!

Recipe for Success!

*A delicious recipe to share with your marketing team!
Feed your soul with good friends, feed your writing with good ideas, feed your stomach with good food.
Keep those creative juices flowing!*

Marketing Mozzarella Salad

Ingredients
- 2 Tbsp balsamic vinegar
- 1 Tbsp olive oil
- 3 mini Persian cucumbers, sliced
- 10-11 cherry tomatoes sliced
- 4-5 Bocconcini small balls of mozzarella cheese, sliced
- Sea salt and freshly cracked pepper to taste

Combine the balsamic vinegar and olive oil together; mix well. Combine the cucumbers, tomatoes, and mozzarella cheese together in a bowl. Season with sea salt and freshly cracked pepper, to taste. Drizzle the top of the salad with the balsamic vinaigrette on top. Serve. Enjoy.

~ Tess Banion
Author: *A Parting Glass – a novel*
Producer of *Garden City* and *I, Too, Sing America: Langston Hughes Unfurled*. http://tessbanion.com/

MARKET YOUR BOOK!
HTTPS://ANAMCARA-PRESS.COM/

> Don't tell me the moon is shining; show me the glint of light on broken glass.
> — Anton Chekhov

Marketing Plan Worksheet

Set Intentions and Determine Tactics & Strategies

Your Book Marketing Plan Assignments

"Marketing ain't easy!" they say. That's why Anamcara Press provides structure and guidance to help authors understand marketing best-practices, and to implement an effective marketing plan, including a written plan to send to book retailers.

In Section I (below) you'll find a detailed description of your seven assignments:

- Gain an Edge
- Find an Audience
- Set Intentions
- Develop Strategies
- Determine Tactics
- Set a Budget
- Establish a Timeline

Consider each carefully and use Section I to guide your answers in Section II.

In Section II you'll fill in the worksheet with your responses for each of the seven assignments. Your completed worksheet—your answers—will become the most important part of your marketing plan.

In Section III you'll turn your worksheet answers into a narrative. The language you provide on the worksheet will be added to the summarized timeline from Chapter 3 to create your complete marketing plan narrative. Don't sweat it if it's not perfect! Getting started is the most important thing.

Section I: Seven Assignments

1. Gaining An Edge

- *You're special!* In one or two paragraphs, describe who you are. What makes you you? You are, in fact, marketing yourself! Describe the highlights of your life, your achievements, your dreams and wishes in Section II below. What organizations are you affiliated with? Where do you donate your time/money? What authors do you follow or books do you read? What makes you tick? What are your tics!?

    Play this game: Name one thing you might say about yourself to others in public; one thing a friend might say about you to others; and one thing a stranger might note about you.•

- *Your book is special!* In one or two paragraphs, describe what makes your book different from the competition. What makes it marketable? And what makes you marketable as its author? Do you have unique credentials? Describe them.

2. Finding Your Target Audience

Who will buy the book? What media outlets do they read, watch, or listen to? If you want to reach "married women with no children and a household income greater than $50,000," say so. The more focused you are, the more likely you are to reach the right audience—those folks who will enjoy your book.

Points to consider when seeking your audience:

- What are the demographics of your ideal readers (age, gender, education, location, etc.)?
- Are there other groups of potential buyers you should target (such as a children's author targeting teachers and parents rather than just trying to appeal to their target readers)?
- What are the primary needs of your target market (and how does your book satisfy those needs)?
- What factors and emotions are likely to influence buying decisions within your target market? You'll want your marketing messages to appeal to those things.

- In what ways, places, or media are your target buyers going to be easiest to reach? (For example, books about grief marketed to *Guidepost* magazine readers, or books about war marketed to veterans.)
- How are authors of similar books describing and promoting their books?

3. Setting Marketing Intentions

An intention is a broad statement of direction that is determined by your needs, wants, and desires. In this case, your intentions are related to marketing your book. With good intentions in place, you can look at each marketing strategy and ask, "Does this step help me achieve my intention?" If the answer isn't "yes," the tactic should be removed from the plan. Intentions are broad but well-defined. They help you stay focused and headed in the right direction.

Sample book marketing intentions.

I intend:

- to develop a fan base that will lead to increased sales of more books in my series.
- to generate book sales through increased visibility in city business journals coast-to-coast. https://www.bizjournals.com/
- to develop relationships with organizations that will post ads in their newsletters about my book.
- to use social media to market my book.
- to find online and actual bookclubs to read my book.
- to use book publicity to generate paid speaking & guest blogging engagements.
- to help position me as an expert in a way that will generate more book sales.

Now create your own!

4. Developing a Strategy

A strategy is your over-arching approach to promoting your book. It's a "big picture" view that summarizes the thinking behind your efforts. What's your strategy for getting exposure for your book? Record it with a bullet point or two.

Here are a few strategy examples to get you thinking:

- To generate pre-release buzz I'll distribute free copies with requests for reviews, and give free copies to people who influence my target audience.
- To focus on public speaking because I sell more books after people hear me speak.
- To do as much marketing online as possible because I'm shy and uncomfortable doing interviews or in-person events.

Your strategy will set the stage for your tactics selection.

5. Determining Tactics

Tactics are the actual steps of your plan. The tactics are the actions you will take to get exposure for your book.

In general, tactics vary from book to book—& should be customized—but the following tactics are used for **all** *books published by Anamcara Press:*

1. Getting pre-publication endorsements (blurbs) or editorial reviews
2. Seeking reader reviews
3. Writing carefully chosen book metadata
4. Writing and distributing a book announcement/press release to print & online media
5. Writing and distributing media kit
6. Creating an author website
7. Creating a landing page for your book
8. Creating an Amazon author page
9. Creating an author Facebook page
10. Creating a Goodreads author page
11. Scheduling book release author events
12. Engaging social media by posting and tweeting pre and post-release

MARKET YOUR BOOK!
HTTPS://ANAMCARA-PRESS.COM/

An author's platform should be established before the book release, and is required by most bookstores & libraries before scheduling an author event.

After the book's release, creative marketing really becomes important.
(Books are typically marketed for three years or more.) Here are more tactics:

- Creating author-written articles based on the book's keywords for media/bloggers/interviewers
- Posting excerpts or teasers
- Creating YouTube videos
- Using Facebook advertising
- Creating a Facebook Live Event
- Using Linked In advertising
- Using Twitter & Instagram effectively
- Creating a Facebook group
- Doing podcast interviews
- Pursuing local, regional, or national media attention
- Writing bylined articles for trade magazines
- Pitching article ideas to the press
- Doing radio interviews
- Blogging as a guest blogger and/or on your website
- Going on a virtual book tour
- Scheduling speaking engagements
- Attending book fairs & festivals
- Seeking awards in book's genre (typically within 1 year of book's release)

Tactics are the tangibles. Selecting the right tactics will help you achieve your intentions. To select the right tactics, ask yourself, "What do I need to do to make my intentions happen?"

Think in terms of specific activities, such as "Write an article for a publication that caters to my target audience," or "Identify influencers on my topic and contact them about writing a pre or post-publication endorsement," or "Use twitter to gain attention for my book's main character."

6. Setting a Budget

When you've finished your list of tactics, consider costs (if any) prioritize your tactics based on value/expense. Implement the tactics you can afford. If your budget is limited, select those you believe will provide the most bang for your buck.

7. Timeline

A timeline will help you manage the strategies and tactics included in your plan. For example, if you want to get pre-publication endorsements, make sure you send requests 3-4 months prior to the books' publication date so that you can add any received to the book's cover and sales page. Planning a virtual book tour? Start building relationships with key bloggers at least six months before your publication date. Review the sample timeline in the first chapter of this book to help develop your book's timeline. *See Chapter 1.*

Pulling It All Together

Once you've reviewed and customized your Author Timeline and completed the Marketing Plan Worksheet, then you're ready to write your book's Marketing Plan Narrative. That narrative can help you get accepted by more book sellers.

Section II: MARKETING PLAN WORKSHEET

Incorporate your strategies & tactics—and all deadlines—into a daily calendar to guide your actions and help you achieve your intentions.

Get started now by completing Section II below.

Complete This Worksheet & Create Language for Your Book Marketing Plan

I know you just wrote a book, and sometimes the tedious task of developing marketing initiatives can feel unnecessary or even futile, but it is the most important first step!

On the next few pages, describe how you will:

1. Gain an Edge
2. Find an Audience
3. Set Intentions
4. Develop Strategy
5. Determine Tactics
6. Set a Budget
7. Follow a Timeline

Directions:

- First, read the assignment descriptions given above in Section I. Let them simmer.
- Second, free-write your responses below—jot down everything you can think of—bullet points are fine! Later you can organize and edit your writing. Get started now:

1. Gain an Edge

I will gain an edge by . . .

2. Find an Audience

Audience 1 _____

Audience 2 _____

Audience 3 _____

3. Set Intentions

Intention 1 _____

Intention 2 _____

Intention 3 _____

MARKET YOUR BOOK!
HTTPS://ANAMCARA-PRESS.COM/

4. Develop Strategy

My over-arching approach to marketing is . . .

5. Determine Tactics

Tactic 1: _____

Tactic 2: _____

Tactic 3: _____

Tactic 4: _____

Tactic 5: _____

Tactic 6: _____

6. Set Budget

Initial costs: $ _____

7. Follow Timeline

Customize the Marketing Plan Timeline from Chapter 1 to fit your book.

Section III: PUTTING IT ALL TOGETHER

Now that you've completed this worksheet & created some language to add to your book's marketing plan, it's time to turn that language from bullet points into paragraphs. The summarized narrative you create below is then added to the Timeline narrative from chapter 3 to create a complete marketing plan.

Use the space below to write your marketing plan from the 7 assignments:

MARKET YOUR BOOK!
HTTPS://ANAMCARA-PRESS.COM/

A professional writer is an amateur who didn't quit.
— Richard Bach

MARKETING QUESTIONNAIRE

1. PRACTICE YOUR PITCH: write a 3 sentence elevator pitch about your book.
_____
_____
_____
_____
_____

2. IMAGINE YOUR READER: describe your reader with 15 keywords:
_____
_____
_____
_____
_____

3. FIND YOUR READERS: where do they go? what do they do?
_____
_____
_____
_____
_____

4. MAP YOUR ROUTE: list your marketing activities so far and where you're headed:
_____
_____
_____
_____
_____
_____

MARKET YOUR BOOK!
HTTPS://ANAMCARA-PRESS.COM/

MAP YOUR ROUTE!

Readers Paradise

COLLABORATION
- Author cooperative
  — write reviews
  — share ideas
- Writing organizations (SF writers of America)

BOOK PROMOTERS
- Goodreads
- Bookbub

ORGANIZATIONS
- Schools
- Libraries
- Bookstores
  — hospitals
  — Historical
  — Gardens

PUBLICATIONS
Magazines & blogs genre specific:
- Guideposts
- Cosmo
- Nature

ADVOCACY GROUPS by topic
- Alcohol
- Disability
- Veterans

SOCIAL MEDIA Content & Links
- Join
- Share
- follow

AUTHOR PLATFORM Content & Links
- Blog
- Share
- follow

You are here
X

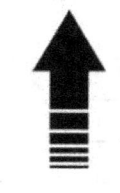

HTTPS://ANAMCARA-PRESS.COM/

MARKETING ACTIVITIES WORKSHEET

Determine Author's Competence & Commitment

SERVICE	MARKETING ACTIVITY	AUTHOR NEEDS NO ASSISTANCE	AUTHOR NEEDS ASSISTANCE
Design & Branding	The most crucial step is the design of the interior and cover of the book. (AC Press does in-house interior and cover design; Chicago Manual of Style followed.)		
Marketing A	Develop metadata: Create Tagline, BISAC Category (Book Industry Standards & Communications category) based on book's genre, Keywords, Book Description, etc.		
Marketing B	Apply marketing metadata		
Marketing C	Author website creation		
Marketing D	Amazon Author Central page		
Marketing E	Webpage on publisher website dedicated to author/book		
Marketing F	Landing Page for Book		
Marketing G	Branded Press Release / media kit, business cards & 4 X 6 book info cards, and Ads for print & for facebook & other social media		
	Press Release - you print yourself		
	Business cards & 4 X 6 cards with your book's details and cover		
	Print and social Media ads (are distributed via email/online)		
Marketing H	Distribute advance reader copies (ARCs) for editorial reviewers		
Marketing I	Social media marketing		
Advertising	Distribute Ads for facebook and other social media pre-release		

MARKET YOUR BOOK!
HTTPS://ANAMCARA-PRESS.COM/

MARKETING ACTIVITIES WORKSHEET, cont.

SERVICE	MARKETING ACTIVITY	AUTHOR NEEDS NO ASSISTANCE	AUTHOR NEEDS ASSISTANCE
Promotion 1	Set up events prior to book's release		
Promotion 2	Contact local and regional booksellers, and national / international booksellers on behalf of book pre-release.		
Promotion 3	Contact local and regional booksellers, and national / international booksellers on behalf of book post-release.		
Promotion 4	Contact local/regional media (radio/TV) on behalf of book pre-release		
Promotion 5	Contact local/regional media (radio/TV) on behalf of book post-release		
Promotion 6	Present book at trade shows and book fairs (e.g. the American Library Association annual conference, etc.)		
Promotion 7	Arrange author signings at events and book fairs (e.g. at the ALA conference)		
Promotion 8	Explore retail placement services to get books into big 4 bookstores		
3rd party Promotion	NetGalley reviews and promotions		
3rd party Promotion	Other paid reviews & promotions		

Once you determine what you can do yourself to market your book, and have reviewed those activities that might require assistance, then you can prioritize what you need assistance with and budget help.

WRITE A MEDIA PITCH

Media & Blog Touring

Put on your scarf and don your gloves, it's time for an internet tour! Approaching editors, reporters, bloggers, TV and radio producers, and talk show hosts is a daunting task—but who better than you to explain what you have to *offer to their audience*? Get ready for a virtual book tour!

Your media kit (sometimes called a press release) is a concise way to provide the most important information about your book on a single printable page to bookstores & libraries. However, it conveys too little information to be helpful for bloggers and interviewers. A better way to pitch the book to those who might interview you and help promote your book is to send what they can actually use on their show/blog immediately.

Media Pitch Writing Guide:

Write a media pitch for your book:

1. Write a short sample article focusing on ONE keyword from your book description.

   SAMPLE KEYWORDS: (e.g.) **addiction; drugs; soldiers; Vietnam War; heroin; trauma**
   - For a newspaper, write a short news story, or a list of tips that address a problem relevant to your book and the selected keyword.
   - For TV and radio, briefly describe the topic you can address in an interview and what you will contribute.

2. Write a few paragraphs introducing yourself and your interest in speaking/being interviewed to send with the article above. Mention any expertise you have in addition to writing your book.

3. Tell media representatives what you have to *offer their audiences*!

Take time to research bloggers and interviewers. What topics does a particular reporter write about? Which editors are in charge of what areas? The more you consider and adjust your article and cover letter to this individual, the better your chances of getting their attention. Are all of the publication's columns and articles staff-written, or do they publish content contributed by readers and free-lancers? Offer to write an author guest-post or submit your article to magazines that accept freelance articles.

Greatest Reach for Your Efforts

Is it more effective to build an audience of 10,000 followers in order to increase book sales, or will encouraging 10 influencers to tell 1,000 of *their* followers to buy your book give better results?

Obviously, you'll get exposure to 10,000 readers faster with the assistance of 10 influencers. Also, the influencer might have more persuasive power to convince others to buy your book than you. An author can only say, "Please buy my new book!" so many times, then an author need to:

- reach out to bloggers
- offer to write a guest blog
- promote other authors and blogs
- comment on other's blog posts
- go on a "blog/media tour"
- join an open submission blogging platform like open salon (https://www.salon.com/2008/08/11/open_salon/)
- network
- keep being creative!

A nickel ain't worth
a dime anymore.
— Yogi Berra

BEWARE!

Writers make three main marketing mistakes:

1. First, we get the goal wrong. Author's often fail to consider their target audience when writing. But authorship requires readership.

2. Second, we go it alone. Writing is a loner activity, and writers are often independent sorts. Joining a writing group or author's cooperative can help—it is like having a companion on the writing trail.

3. Third, we fail to plan ahead. Like a hiker, you need your writer's backpack filled with useful stuff—both physical and metaphorical—to reach the summit of writing for readers. Those tools include a solid author platform to stand on, a publishing route mapped out, companion authors, knowledge of the obstacles and how to overcome them, and a clear vision of the audience you intend to reach.

From: *A Good Climb*— read the full article here: https://anamcara-press.com/traveling-in-books-without-cars/

Watch out for rip-offs!

1. "We'll put your book on display" at a conference or book fair. Only $500.
   This service is not worth your money. You'd be better off to pay for a table (usually about $150- 300) and transportation to the conference and sell your book yourself! While it is great to have your book displayed at a book fair, if you're not there to push it and/or the book is not represented in a catalog, it is practically invisible among the many others on display.

2. "We'll publicize your book" by developing your promotional materials. Only $5,000.
   This usually means creating the metadata that you have worked so hard already to develop if you've followed the steps in this book. Services offered are typically what you see listed above in the 21 steps. (Some publicists will offer media marketing—a service that promises a guaranteed number of appearances or interviews. That service is not listed above, and might be valuable.)

3. "We'll develop your website and social media platform." Only $4,999 or $250 a month forever.
   While an author platform that includes a website and social media presence is necessary, spending 4K is not! Hire a kid instead. I recently had a salesman push a $250 per month website subscription at me. Just say no. You've got this!

Authors need to consider the most effective marketing tasks—and their budget—before investing time or money. We need to develop good marketing habits, and also beware of those who would scam us!

MARKET YOUR BOOK!
HTTPS://ANAMCARA-PRESS.COM/

Recipe for Success!

*A delicious recipe to share with your marketing team!
Feed your soul with good friends, feed your writing with good ideas, feed your stomach with good food. Keep those creative juices flowing!*

Worksheet Gluten-Free Sheetcake

Ingredients
1 1/4 cups brown rice flour
1 cup almond flour
3/4 cups maple syrup
2 teaspoons baking powder
1/2 teaspoon baking soda
1/4 teaspoon salt
1/4 cup softened butter
1 cup almond milk
1/4 cup butter canola oil
3 large eggs
1 1/2 teaspoons vanilla extract
buttercream frosting

Preheat oven to 350 degrees F. Grease a 9x13-inch pan
Whisk together dry ingredients salt in a large bowl. Blend softened butter and maple syrup. Mix, on medium speed, until butter is incorporated.
Add the milk, oil, egg yokes, and vanilla extract. Mix until batter is smooth and fluffy, about one minute. Beat egg whites until stiff and fold in last.

Spread batter evenly into greased pan. Bake until a cake tester inserted in the center comes out clean, about 30 minutes. Frost cooled cake with your buttercream frosting.

~ M Carroll
Author: *Photographer, Paratrooper, POW: A Wyoming Cowboy in Hitler's Germany*
https://maureencarroll.com/

EBook Focused Strategy

Chapter 5

Tried and True eBook Strategies to Review

The best strategies are the ones that work for you! What does your time and budget allow? Now that you've carefully reviewed seven concepts of marketing yourself and your book, and detailed your marketing timeline, you're ready for deeper consideration of book sales strategies.

EBooks are less expensive, and often easier for folks to read and carry than print books. An eBook focused strategy can increase initial Amazon and Goodreads reviews, and thereby sales. For Indie books, the eBook is usually released at the same time as the paperback. You can pre-release both print and eBook on Amazon to increase notice & gather both sales and reviews after the release date. Here's an example strategy:

EBook Focused Strategy

Email list & Netgalley Pre-Release

- Ask people on your email list to be "first readers" of your new book.
- Prior to publication upload your book to NetGalley, a community where librarians, bloggers, educators, booksellers and media can read your book for potential reviews and recommendations. https://www.netgalley.com/

Book Bloggers Pre and Post-Release

- the Indie View - awesome list of reviewers, organized by genre (http://www.theindieview.com/indie-reviewers/)
- The Book Blogger List - free directory of book reviewers, organized by genre (http://bookbloggerlist.com/)

Discount Review Sites Post Release

STEP ONE:
- Bookbub
- Freebooksy
- ENT
- RobinReads
- Fussy Librarian
- My Book Cave
- more listed on page 36 with links

MARKET YOUR BOOK!
HTTPS://ANAMCARA-PRESS.COM/

GET REVIEWS FOR YOUR EBOOK PRE-RELEASE

Your mission is to gain fifty legitimate Amazon reviews in six weeks. That, dear Author, is a big goal, and for most authors unattainable. Focus on getting 10 reviews, as this is the threshold where most paid promo sites allow you to advertise. Be brave and persistent and follow these 10 steps:

1. Grow thick skin. Honest reviews can be painful. Use feedback wisely. Try to dismiss mean or overly-picky feedback, and contemplate constructive criticism as this will help you hone your writing skills.

2. Send your print or eBook to editorial reviewers. You'll need to send out your book three to four months before launch. Include a cover letter and your book's media kit. Follow the reviewers posted guidelines regarding how many copies to send in the desired format, in the required time-frame. Make sure you include a self-addressed stamped envelop, and don't expect the print copies of your book to be returned. *See list of editorial reviewers in the appendix.*

3. Ask the people on your email list to be your book's first readers. Explain the importance of their feedback—even though they're amateurs—and include a review form for them to fill out. Don't incentivize people in any way; this is against the rules. Just ask nicely in a newsletter or include the request as a "PS" at the bottom of your emails with the subject line "Can You Do Me a Favor?"

4. Amateur reviewers fall into three categories: (1) silent - they will give you no feedback. Never mind. (2) editors - they will offer editing advice and find types. Thank them. (3) reviewers - these are people that will give you honest feedback about the content of your book. Listen to them.

5. After getting feedback from your email list, select favorable comments to sprinkle on your website, and some even inside your book! Seek permission from the blurb's authors, and request that they put their comments (review) on Amazon or Goodreads on the date of the book's release.

6. On the release date, send a reminder email to Amateur-reviewers to leave their comments on Amazon & Goodreads. Only those who have spent a specified, minimum amount on Amazon's site, and are not deemed by Amazon to be "close friends or relatives" may successfully leave reviews. Because of Amazon's strict review policy, close friends and colleagues (and Facebook friends) may not be able to leave a review on Amazon for your book.

7. Ask those unable to leave reviews on Amazon to leave their review on Goodreads, and other reader websites. The feedback readers give to the author is valuable even if they are not able to leave a review.

8. Reminder email. Wait 3 days and send out a reminder email. In this email thank everyone who has left a review and thank people in advance who haven't posted yet.

9. Final Call: Similar to the previous email, reminding people the book is live and is ready for a review.

10. Don't forget to add your eBook's URL to your email signature, to your social media sites, and to your website!

Sample Message For Editorial Reviewers:

Subject: Book Title by Author

Dear Editor, Describe your book in 1-2 sentences. Provide information about your book in the form of a Media Kit. Provide a link to your website/book page, and 1-2 sentences about you as the author. Finally, provide them with a copy of your eBook or PDF for possible review if you're sending an email (check the reviewers requirements), or send them the requisite number of paperback books with printed cover letter and media kit, and stamped self-addressed envelop.

Sample Message For Amateur Reviewers:

Subject: Can you do me a favor?

Dear Name of person, Describe your book in 1-2 sentences and ask them if they'd be willing to read your book and give you some feedback about it. Ask if they want to receive a PDF, e-book, or paperback to read and review. Give them a deadline.

Paid Reviews

There are services that offer unbiased editorial book reviews for a fee. The most well-known is Kirkus Reviews. From their website: *"Kirkus has been a premiere marketing vehicle for the top publishing houses in America, reviewing their books and building early buzz for new releases. Its robust audience of both consumers and industry professionals, spanning from librarians and booksellers to publishers and film executives, has been as instrumental in drawing attention to debut authors as it has been in launching major bestsellers."*

- Kirkus Reviews (https://www.kirkusreviews.com/)

A Kirkus review may be placed on your website, on your book cover, and in your metadata. However, it is not an Amazon review. There are paid review services that will find reviewers who will review (legitimately) on Amazon. They do this for a fee, but it is not the same as buying reviews for your book which violates Amazon's review policy. Amazon has taken action against thousands of sites that were selling incentivized reviews (e.g. *I'll give you a book or $ if you'll leave a review*), and removed those reviews from author's book pages. Real review services can find reviewers for your book without incurring Amazon's wrath. The most influential site is *NetGalley*.

NetGalley

NetGalley can be used both pre- and post-publication. Around 500,000 reviewers, bloggers, librarians, booksellers, educators, and media professionals worldwide use the site to discover new books, make buying decisions and leave feedback for publishers and authors. You can list your book and hope readers find it, but you will get lots more reviewers if you have a plan to promote your book.

NetGalley has a marketing program, and a widget you can place on your website. You can email your contact list or reach out to book bloggers with a link to your book (many book bloggers are registered members of NetGalley).

To put a book on NetGalley, authors first need to complete a contract and submit payment. Authors can select from the basic six-month listing option, and the Marketing-Plus-Title listing which includes placement in the NetGalley Newsletter.

Here is a link to an informational NetGalley video: https://www.youtube.com/watch?v=ZE5OJ5LY67U

Other Paid Review Sites

Here is a list of paid review sites that offer an opportunity for honest reviews for your book. You aren't purchasing reviews per se, instead, these sites play matchmaker between authors and prospective reviewers—matching your book with interested, unbiased reviewers who request a review copy of your book based on the cover, blurb, and genre.

- City Book Review (https://citybookreview.com/)
- Hidden Gems (https://www.hiddengemsbooks.com/)
- KO's Stuffed Shelf (https://stuffedshelf.com/)
- Library Thing (https://www.librarything.com/)
- Vine Reviews (https://www.amazon.com/gp/vine/help). Vine Reviews accepts up to 30 reviews for your Amazon book page. The author may **not** contact reviewers, unlike NetGalley which has no limit and encourages authors to communicate with reviewers.

OFFER PROMOTIONAL DISCOUNTS POST-RELEASE

Use Kirkus, your email list, and NetGalley pre-release. Post-release, use book bloggers and eBook discounted marketing websites, and book promotion discount sites to increase Amazon & Goodreads reviews & sales.

Set a budget for book promotions before you begin. Use the following list to get started; book promotion sites are organized from most to least worthwhile. Be prepared to sell your book for free or $0.99. Never do this at launch, only post-release.

Most sites list books by genre (e.g. fantasy or mystery), they often don't list sub-genres. If your book doesn't fit neatly into a specified genre, be aware this can mess with Amazon's algorithms.

Offer your post-release eBook for $0.99 for the first promotional event. Six months (or more) later, run another promotional event offering the book for free. This process allows you to target a different subscriber base each time.

If you don't want to schedule your own book promotions, you can hire a service (for a fee) to take on this important marketing task for you.

- Book Rank: submits your book for you to sites of your choosing

    (https://www.book-rank.com/)

Three Rules

There are three rules to follow when using paid promotional sites:

- Use them for book releases or to support BookBubs/Kindle Countdown Deals for books post-release.
- Use multiple sites for short periods of time. Combine this with other marketing tools like your email list, newsletter, and paid ads.
- Don't use the same service more than once every six months. Wait a year before using a site for the same book again. This does not apply to Bookbub—but they'll only run the same book once every six months, anyway.

The goal is to find the happy-place on Amazon's Algorithms. You want sales in adequate numbers (many per week) for a long enough period (several weeks) for the algorithms to activate and start recommending the book to the rest of the Amazon world. To achieve this, use many sites, at least on the final two days of your promotion efforts in order to achieve maximum impact.

eBOOK DISCOUNTED PROMOTION WEBSITES

BOOKBUB	https://www.bookbub.com/partners	(price varies): BookBub beats every site on this list by many orders of magnitude.
FREEBOOKSY	https://www.freebooksy.com/	($50 – $100): the best site for free books outside of BookBub
ENT	http://www.ereadernewstoday.com/	($35 – $60)
ROBINREADS	https://robinreads.com/	($30 – $85)
FUSSY LIBRARIAN	https://www.thefussylibrarian.com/	($10 – $30): account required
MY BOOK CAVE	https://mybookcave.com/	($15): account required
BARGAIN BOOKSY	https://www.bargainbooksy.com/	($25 – $80): FreeBooksy's sister site for paid books; not nearly as powerful, but still solid
BOOK BARBARIAN & BOOK ADRENALINE	https://bookbarbarian.com/ https://bookadrenaline.com/	($35 – $55): SF/Fantasy only & related site for thrillers/mysteries.
BOOKBUZZ	http://bookbuzz.net/30-day-blitz-on-30-websites-blogs-newsletters/	Book promos and NetGalley
BOOKGORILLA	https://www.bookgorilla.com/	a daily email service that informs readers about quality ebooks at great prices

- *pricing current as of the publication of this book.*

Recipe for Success!

A delicious recipe to share with your marketing team!
Feed your soul with good friends, feed your writing with good ideas, feed your stomach with good food.

Keep those creative juices flowing!

Co-Author Cherry Upside Down Cake

Ingredients
1 Yellow Cake Mix (and ingredients to make batter as directed on box)
1 Can Cherry Filling
1 Tsp. Almond Flavoring
1/4 Cup Margarine
3/4 Cup Brown Sugar

Coat a bundt pan with a cooking spray like Pam
Melt margarine and stir in brown sugar
Add almond flavoring to cherry pie filling and add
Pour into the bunt pan
Make cake batter according to directions on box and pour over cherry mixture in bundt pan
Use a knife to cut through batter once

Bake according to cake directions on box, checking for doneness by inserting a toothpick into the cake to ensure it comes out clean.

Let cool in the pan for 30 minutes and then invert onto a plate.
Enjoy!

~ Vicki Julian
Author: *Simple Things to Make This World a Better Place*, and contributor to the *Chicken Soup for the Soul* Series
http://www.vickijulian.com/

Online Marketing Plan of Action

A written marketing plan for your book is the first step in reaching your target audience. The next step is putting that plan into action.

NEXT STEPS: Creating Good Marketing Habits

You've completed a your written marketing plan for your book. That is a major accomplishment, one that many dream of but few achieve. Now it's time to get to work on activating that plan.

Marketing your book needs to become habitual, something you do routinely like brushing your teeth.

Automation helps to make the task easier, however, someone still has to create that content and send that tweet! You can choose to do your own social media marketing with zero assistance because you're an expert. Or a social media manager can provide regular assistance to get the message out about your book and create events. Or something in-between.

What is your level of assistance needed with the following:

Social Media	Email	Website
Set Up Social Media Accounts; Set Up Calendar & Add Important Dates; Create and/or add content; Set Up Automated Messaging	Create email Ad for Social Media Event; Determine Dates of Distribution; Set Up Automated Messaging (Mailchimp is useful)	Create/update author website &/or blog page; create and/or post content; automate blog posts

4 Social Media Marketing Strategies to Share

Social Media Marketing

The best strategies are the ones that work for you! What does your time and budget allow? Now that you've reviewed good marketing habits, it's time to get started on the most important and impactful strategy for marketing your book: *social media marketing*.

Social media marketing steps 1 through 4, below, are interwoven. After your accounts for Facebook, Twitter, Linked In, and Instagram, etc. are established, then your calendar is set up & dates are selected for posting. Posts about physical, in-person events are scheduled and repeated 2-3 times, *this is where automation is handy*. Software services like Mailchimp can help you create & automate email and social media posts. There are other automation software programs including *Buffer* & *Sprout* that you can add to your website if you prefer. *The important thing is to post regularly in order to build your audience!*

Social Media Marketing Steps

Set Up Social Media Accounts
- Facebook
- Instagram
- Twitter
- Linked In
- Pinterest
- Other

Set Up Calendar & Add Important Dates
- Create/update calendar adding author events related to book
- Update Calendar adding author events unrelated to book

Create and/or Add Content
- Find/create content
- Create social media posts based on event or creative content
- Customize content for platform (Facebook add graphics, Twitter limited number of words, etc.)

Set Up Automated Messaging
- Determine number of times content to be shared
- Share to social media accounts (Facebook, Twitter, etc.)
- Schedule date/time & number of posts

Select the level of assistance you'll need with the following:

Getting your book's social media marketing in shape is a challenging task! There is assistance available to help authors complete social media and marketing tasks, including setting up social media accounts, setting up a calendar of important dates, and automating social media messaging to get the word out.

There are 2 important tasks you need to do every week (preferably twice per week!)

- create content for your platform (your platform includes your website & social media accounts)
- Post on your website & social media

Social media posting and blogging are things you need to make habitual. Do yourself, or seek assistance with the following tasks:

- determine best social media accounts to sign up for
- sign up for accounts
- automate account postings through software
- create inspiring posts relevant to your book's marketing strategies and branding
- create automated, regular blog postings

Readers love to put quotes on Twitter and Facebook so give them little bites of wisdom from your book, or interesting tidbits about characters that they can easily share with their friends.

A little buzz goes a long way. Active authors gain fans. If you're not active, folks don't know about you or your book. With a gazillion books available on Amazon today, keeping active on social media, collecting Amazon & Goodreads reviews, and continuing to write and blog are the most effective ways to spend your book-marketing time.

3 Email Marketing Strategies to Engage In

Email Marketing

Email marketing continues to be an important strategy in your marketing plan. We all read email messages most everyday. Creating attention-grabbing headlines and memorable content is key to making email marketing work for your book sales.

In general, email messaging should be distributed far less frequently than social media postings, and be more news focused. However, email messages should be regular and targeted (as much as possible.) Email postings will typically be about book publication and event dates, as well as calls to action—*like please leave a review!*

Email marketing includes creating email ads for events, determining dates of distribution, and setting up automated email messaging to get the word out. When you have important announcements, your message should be emailed to your list. Make sure you include a link to your book, and a request for them to leave a review of your book on the book review site of their choice. Add a PS at the end asking them to share the email with friends.

Email Marketing Steps

Create Email Ad for Social Media or Physical Event

- Determine audience
- Add content
- Create ad

Determine Dates of Distribution

- Events related to book - 3x prior & 1 x after event
- Book fairs & festivals where book will be displayed - 3x prior
- Author events unrelated to book

Set Up Automated Messaging

- Automate distribution of advertisements based on calendar of events

MARKET YOUR BOOK!
HTTPS://ANAMCARA-PRESS.COM/

Persistance can look a lot like stupid.
— Kristen Lamb,
Are You There Blog? It's Me, Writer

3 Blogging Strategies to Brag About

Website Marketing

Website marketing is the base requirement for any marketing plan. It is the first thing that pops up when people search your name (hopefully), and can communicate and share your message. Just as your eyes are the window to your soul, your website is the window to your authorship. When you blog you let others get to know you as an author. Fans appreciate getting to know authors personally. Bottom line: create a website & get to blogging!

Complete the following website marketing tasks: create your author website blog page; determine your blogging schedule; set up automated blogs to get the word out about your writing. ***Keep in mind you can blog on websites other than your own!***

Blogging Steps

Create Author Website Blog Page | Create Blog Content | Determine Blogging Schedule & Set Up Automated Blogs

- Create website
- Create blog page
- Set up seo
- Set up categories
- Add keywords

- Create content
- *Create blogs about all events*
- *Create blogs about all book fairs & festivals author attends*
- *Create blogs about author events unrelated to book*

- Schedule blog date/time
- Spread out to keep content consistent and regular
- Add in the extra one now and again for the element of surprise!

Recipe for Success!

A delicious recipe to share with your marketing team!
Feed your soul with good friends, feed your writing with good ideas, feed your stomach with good food. Keep those creative juices flowing!

Ebook Deviled Eggs

Ingredients
12 large free-range eggs
4 tbsp mayonnaise
1–2 tsp mustard
1 tsp salt
¼ paprika, plus extra for sprinkling
few drops Tabasco
2 tbsp olive oil
2–3 tbsp water
2 tsp finely chopped chives

Bring some water to the boil and add the eggs, returning the water to boil. Boil for 1 minute, then turn the heat off and leave the eggs to stand in the pan for 12 minutes. Cool, and rinse in cold water for peeling ease.

Pop the yokes out into a bowl and add the mayonnaise, a teaspoon of English mustard, the salt and paprika to the egg yolks, and shake a few drops of Tabasco on top. Mash with a fork, then add the oil and blend until smooth. It will be very thick. Stir in as much of the water as needed for consistency.

Fill egg whites and sprinkle with paprika and chopped chives.

~ M Carroll
Author: Spiders Dance
https://maureencarroll.com/

MARKET YOUR BOOK!
HTTPS://ANAMCARA-PRESS.COM/

YouTube Marketing

3 YouTube Strategies to Adopt

You've written a book, created a website & blog page, and created an author page on Amazon & Goodreads. You've set up social media accounts on Instagram, Facebook, Twitter, and others. You're blogging and posting about things related to your book (and your writing & projects in general.) Email messages are flying with announcements about your book's release and post-release events. Keep smiling. It's time for a YouTube video!

Short, shorter, and shortest YouTube videos are a great way to get your book noticed. Longer, informational videos that are focused on one or more of your books keywords can also be great marketing tools. Just as writing short articles based on your keywords can help market you to bloggers and other interviewers, YouTube videos can introduce your book to a wider audience.

YouTube Marketing Steps

Write Content

- Prior to filming, spend some time considering the content of your YouTube video. Write for a listener rather than a reader.
- Practice your introduction and book description language outloud.
- Get feedback from others

Create Videos

- 90 second promo
- 3 minute promo
- 15-20 minute instructional video—what will they learn?

Sprinkle YouTube Videos Across Social Media

- Add video to Website
- Amazon author page
- Share on Facebook
- Share on other social media sites
- Email video to email list

MARKET YOUR BOOK!
HTTPS://ANAMCARA-PRESS.COM/

Recipe for Success!

A delicious recipe to share with your marketing team!
Feed your soul with good friends, feed your writing with good ideas, feed your stomach with good food. Keep those creative juices flowing!

NetGalley Spicy Navy & Spinach Bean Soup

Ingredients:
1 Medium size Onion
½ lb Spinach
1 Green Bell Pepper
1 Medium size Onion
½ lb Spinach
2 cups Navy beans
1 cup of black beans rinsed off
2 15 oz cans Habanero diced tomatoes
1 Red Bell Pepper
32 oz of water or chicken broth

In large pan pour in Water or chicken broth heat on stove in medium high temperature.

Drain and rinse Navy and Black Beans the put in pan with liquid bring to boil slowly.

Cut Onion into wedges put in pan.
Slice Peppers in thin long strips put in pan.
Pour in Habanero diced tomatoes.

Once liquid is boiling place the Spinach in and slow boil for 6 minutes and serve. Makes twelve servings.

~ Perry Shepard
Author: *The Hero Versus Me & Monkey Jo*
https://perryshepard.com/

Paid Online Advertising

Much of online advertising is free for the sharing, but paid advertising has a place in your marketing plan, too.

Facebook, Amazon, Online Rags

You've shared your Facebook posts, but only some of your friends interacted. That's because only some of your friends saw the post in their feed. In fact, it may not have posted to their feed at all!

Facebook uses algorithms to behind-the-scenes, electronically guide posts to interested users. Many have tried to crack the code. Unless you're some wiz of a programmer, it's probably easier and more effective to pay for Facebook marketing.

Amazon paid ads also have a role in helping to place your book in front of prospective readers when they are searching for something similar (but don't know about your book yet.)

Your book sales may also benefit from ads placed in online magazines who target readers in general and/or your book's topic specifically.

Facebook Paid Ads	Amazon Paid Ads	Online Rags Paid Ads
Boost your posts	Create ads for Amazon	Create ads for print & online magazines

Share Wider with Facebook Ads

Facebook Paid Advertising

Complete the following Facebook marketing tasks: create an author page and Facebook advertisements, determine posting schedule, and set up automated posts to get the word out.

Posts can be created in Mailchimp and customized for each social media platform. Once a post is shared to a Facebook page, any author can share the ad to their own Facebook page. Authors can help each other out by sharing each other's posts! Once posted, the post can be boosted for a fee charged by Facebook. This will enable your post to reach a wider audience.

Facebook is set up to let you post paid ads through your Facebook Author page. First you'll need to select a budget and determine how long the ad will run. When running paid ads it's best to track your results.

Facebook Advertising Steps

1 — Create Facebook Ads
- Follow Facebook ad Guidelines
- Post ads on the right day/time
- Track ads results

2 — Share Facebook Ads
- Share ads in relevant Facebook groups
- Start your own Facebook group; share

3 — Practice Good Karma
- Share other author's Facebook ads & spread the word about other author's books you love!
- You're more noticed on FB the more you like & share!

MARKET YOUR BOOK!
HTTPS://ANAMCARA-PRESS.COM/

Create More Buzz with Amazon Ads

Amazon Paid Advertising

Amazon is set up to let you post paid ads through your Amazon Author page. First you'll need to select a budget and determine how long the ad will run. When running paid ads it's best to track your results.

Authors can benefit by setting up Amazon ads and develop branded advertising on the Amazon platform. Consider the following when running paid ads on Amazon:

Amazon Advertising Steps

Keywords

- Gather 300 relevant keywords
- Look at similar book's keywords
- Do a synonym search

Use Small Budgets

- Modest bids in multiple campaigns are most effective
- Under $10 per day
- Be patient—it may take two weeks for a sale to register

Get Creative!

- Clicks but no sales means the ad is attracting the wrong people. Double check the relevance of your keywords
- No clicks means campaign is not resonating. It may not be the ad, however, as Amazon can be erratic. With two identical ads one may skyrocket and the other fizzle. Run new ad.

Recipe for Success!

*A delicious recipe to share with your marketing team!
Feed your soul with good friends, feed your writing with good ideas, feed your stomach with good food. Keep those creative juices flowing!*

Headway Hummus

Ingredients:
2 cans chickpeas, drain and save the liquid
1/4 cup tahini
1/4 cup lemon juice
2 cloves garlic minced or pressed
1/2 tsp cumin powder
1/2 tsp salt
parsley for garnish

Place the chickpeas, tahini, lemon, garlic, cumin, and salt in a blender or food processor. Blend until smooth, adding additional lemon juice as needed for consistency. Season to taste and garnish with parsley, olive oil, and olives as desired. Serve with pita bread or crackers.

Margaret Kramar
Author: *Searching for Spenser*
http://www.margaretkramar.com/

MARKET YOUR BOOK!
HTTPS://ANAMCARA-PRESS.COM/

Paid Print Advertising

Much of print advertising is costly, but paid advertising has a place in your marketing plan, too.

Is Print Advertising Dead?

In spite of social media, we still meet face to face and interact in person and up close most every day. We exchange greetings, and other things, like more information about each other on business cards and flyers. Print advertising isn't dead—it's just kind of sleepy compared to social media advertising.

There are ways that print advertising rivals online advertising. For example, print advertising allows three or more points of contact with a prospective buyer: when they receive the print material (you hand them your card), later when they pick it up again after putting it in a bag, wallet, or pocket ("Oh, yeah. Sam has a book out"), and potentially again before they toss it in the trash or go online to order your book! With email and social media there is usually just one point of contact—they see your post right before they delete the message or search for you/your book online. Another way print rivals online advertising is by the connection with *you*! They remember your smile, or the conversation that led up to receiving your card.

Book Business Cards	Book/Author 3X5 Cards	Print Rags Paid Ads
Carry them everywhere and give them out freely!	Give at events to those who express interest but don't buy then. Leave at local businesses.	Find magazines relevant to your genre. Write articles for the magazine's audience. See sample ad below

Sample Print Ad

"Margaret Kramar's memoir is a testament to the pain and beauty of parenthood—and the vulnerability it requires." —Laura Moriarty, best selling author of *The Chaperone*, and *American Heart*.

Parenting can be a struggle; especially parenting a disabled child. In this flawlessly written memoir, Kramar describes championing her son, diagnosed with Sotos syndrome, through his short life. She examines the experience of loving and losing a child and reminds us that there is a way forward through the grief. Kramar's memoir offers guidance, wisdom and inspiration. An amazing story of redemption and hope.

"This book is a reminder that living with a most difficult and painful thing gives us choices. Making the right one makes all the difference. Margaret Kramar has written this story for all the right reasons. And no matter who you are, you will find yourself in these pages."

—MARYEMMA GRAHAM, UNIVERSITY OF KANSAS DISTINGUISHED PROFESSOR & FOUNDER/DIRECTOR, PROJECT ON THE HISTORY OF BLACK WRITING

BIOGRAPHY/AUTOBIOGRAPHY
DISABILITIES/PHYSICAL CHALLENGES
FAMILY CARE/PARENTING

WINNER OF THE NATIONAL INDIE EXCELLENCE AWARD 2019

Margaret Kramar is an educator and taught English at the University of Kansas where she completed her PhD in the areas of modernism, autobiography and disability studies. Kramar's creative nonfiction has most recently appeared in *Joy Interrupted: An Anthology on Motherhood and Loss* and *Echoes from the Prairie*. http://www.margaretkramar.com/

ANAMCARA PRESS LLC
PO Box 442072, Lawrence KS 66044-2072, (785) 843-1849

Anamcara Press
anamcara-press.com/

Direct Sales

Sell Yourself and Your Book Directly

Direct sales marketing requires you to really put yourself out there. Are you willing to sell your book directly to strangers? Will you carry your book and 3 x 5 card with your book's information everywhere? Will you call bookstores on behalf of your book? That's direct sales.

Cold calls are a hard task for most authors. Calling bookstores and libraries is time consuming and ego-deflating. While some authors are steeled for the task, others may prefer to hire out cold-calling to an expert to help get their book presented to libraries and bookstores.

Begin locally, then broaden your efforts; contact bookstores, libraries, and media outlets to get the word out about you and your book. *You'll find a list of bookstores, libraries, and media in the appendix.*

Note: your book must have a distributable ISBN (International Standard Book Number) in order to market your book to bookstores and libraries.

Direct Sales Steps

Contact Bookstores

- Review list of bookstores
- Select relevant bookstores
- Contact event manager

Contact Libraries

- Review list of libraries
- Select relevant libraries
- Contact acquisitions manager
- Contact event manager

Contact Media (TV/radio, magazines, bookclubs)

- Determine contact information
- Contact appropriate person
- Follow their procedures for setting up interviews

MARKET YOUR BOOK!
HTTPS://ANAMCARA-PRESS.COM/

Recipe for Success!

A delicious recipe to share with your marketing team! Feed your soul with good friends, feed your writing with good ideas, feed your stomach with good food. Keep those creative juices flowing!

Pre-Launch Chili Pie

1 package pre-made pie crust
2 cups colby jack cheese shredded
1 oz can diced green chili drained
1/4 tsp chili powder
1 cup salsa

Allow crust to thaw. Heat oven to 450 unfold one crust onto ungreased cookie sheet. Sprinkle cheese over crust within 1/2 inch of edges. Sprinkle with green chilies. Unfold remaining crust. Place over the other and pinch the edges together. Generously prick the top with fork. Sprinkle with chili powder.

Bake at 450 for 10-15 minutes until golden brown. Let stand 5 minutes. Cut into wedges. Serve with salsa.

~ Mishea Obiji
Author / Illustrator: *The Secret of the Magic Crystal*
https://obijiart.com/

MARKET YOUR BOOK!
HTTPS://ANAMCARA-PRESS.COM/

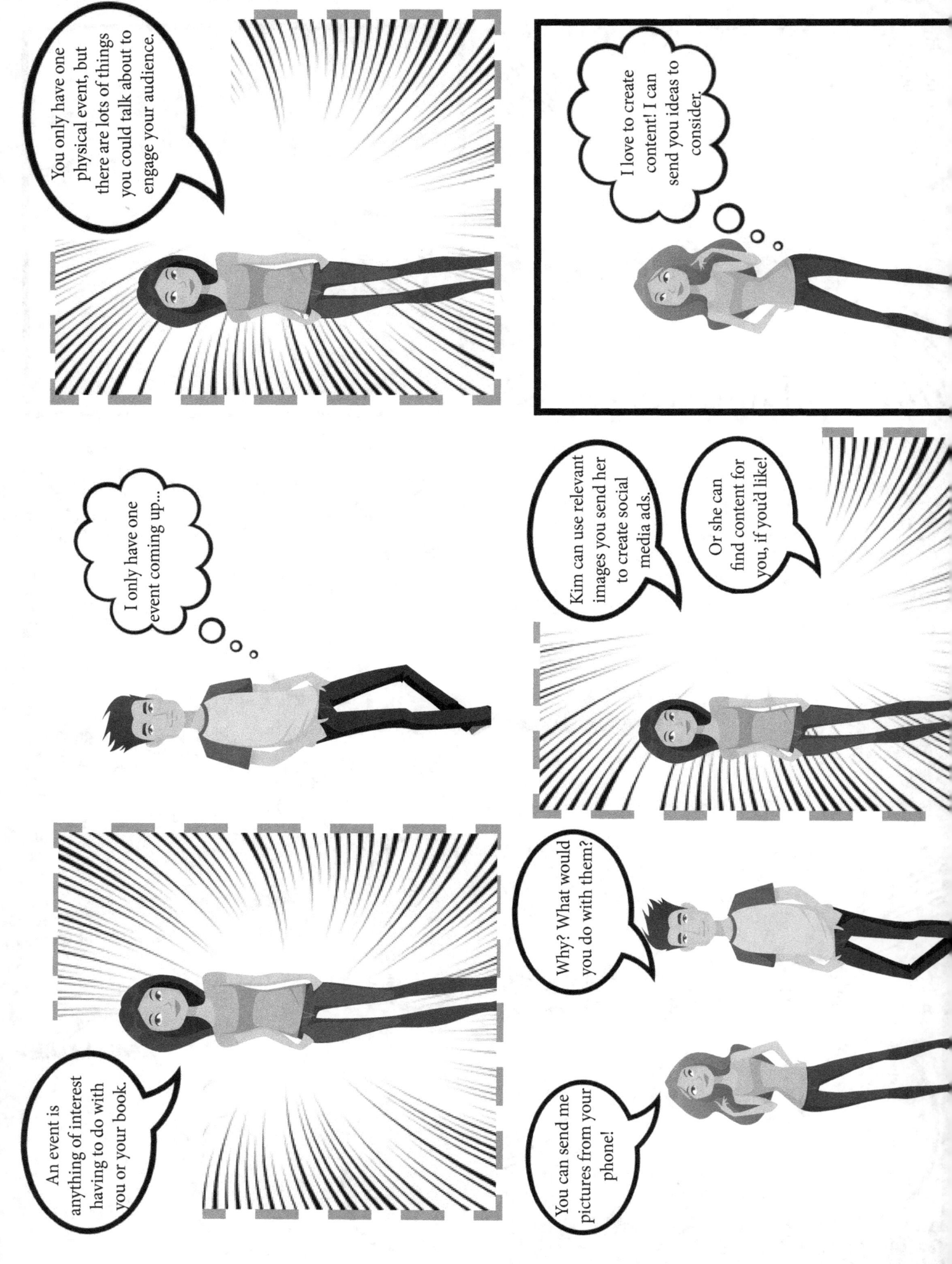

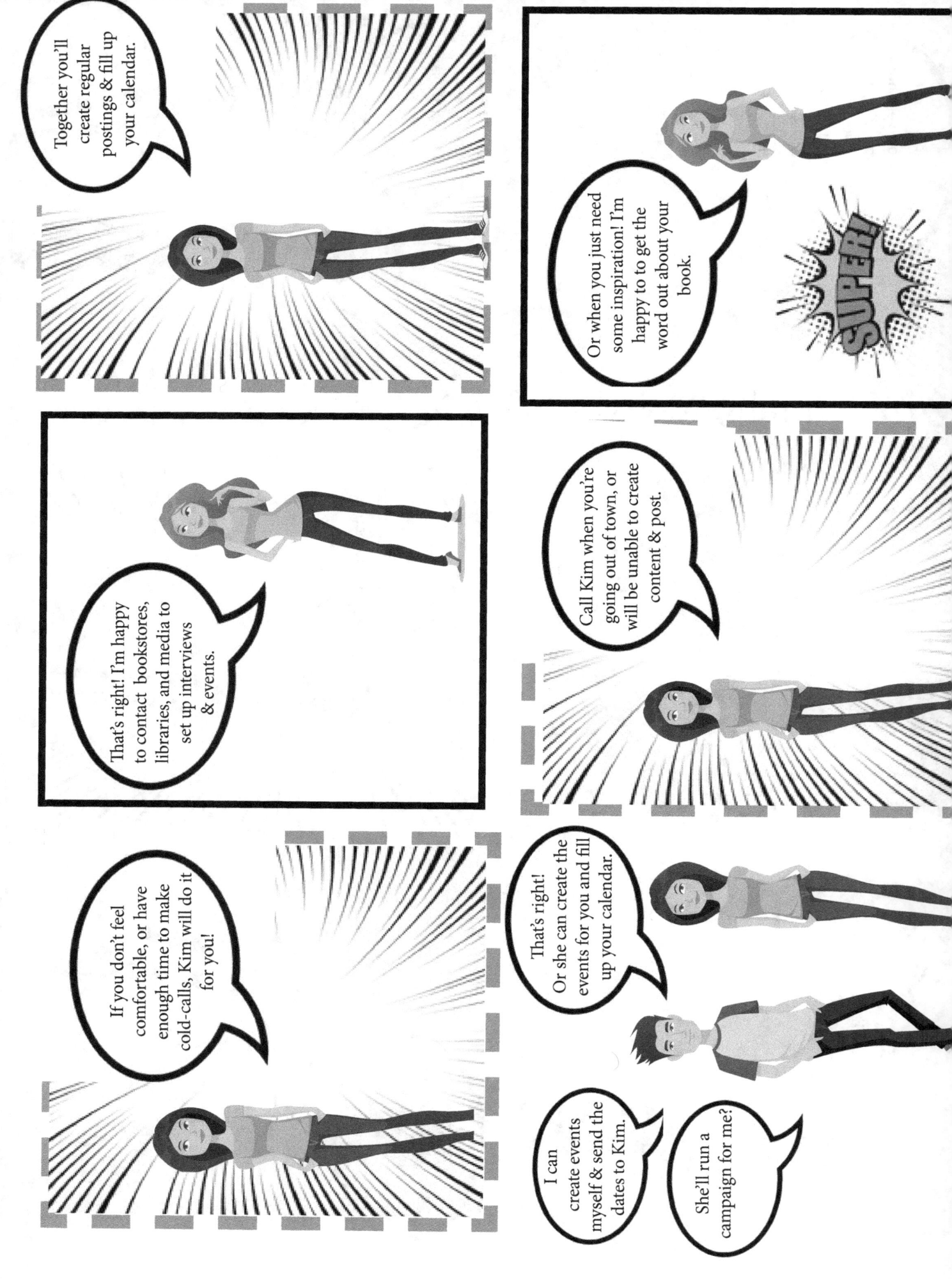

Count Down!

Prepare for your book's launch

You've completed your marketing worksheet & drafted your book's marketing plan. You've learned the difference between editorial and amateur reviewers, slogged through social media marketing strategies and email strategies. You've practiced your pitch, defined your target audience, and mapped your marketing route. You've written a media kit and have ideas of where to send it.

You've also taken a hard look at yourself and assessed your competence and commitment to marketing and determined where you need help. You know the importance of blogging and developing good social media marketing habits overall. You're now ready to prepare for your book's launch. Congratulations!

Launch Steps

3 - 6 Months in Advance

- Build your author platform including website and book landing page.
- Submit your book for editorial review.
- Contact organizations to schedule launch events and plan your book tour.
- Contact media & bloggers for interviews or hire a PR firm.

(PR firms listed in the appendix)

1 - 3 Months in Advance

- Complete your book's description page and author profile on Amazon.
- Use NetGalley to get reviews.
- Join Goodreads and get active.
- Send two promotional emails per week to your email list with book snippets & excerpts.
- Speak in public and/or conduct live videos on Facebook, Livestream, etc.

Launch Week

- Begin your book tour, including local book signings, or public speaking events.
- Continue to send promotional emails weekly to your email list with book snippets and teasers.

MARKET YOUR BOOK!
HTTPS://ANAMCARA-PRESS.COM/

Resources

Follow up on your marketing knowledge

This little book is just an appetizer! Marketing is a big, broad, deep, and ever changing subject that could be studied for years! Most authors would rather leave marketing to the experts, but selling our books requires gaining at least some basic understanding of how and why marketing works. That's why there are additional marketing resources for authors in the appendix of this book.

Marketing strategies and tactics change all of the time. We live in a changing world with changing technology. Since the beginning of the 21st Century we have seen the advent of GPS, social networking, the touch screen, mobile operating systems, artificial hearts, and YouTube!

It's not like marketing your book isn't daunting enough. Once you figure out some strategy—"Hey! I can do this Facebook thing!"—then the technology changes and you get to learn something new. It's not all bad news—this technology changin' thing can keep us agile in the noggin. There is other good news in the form of helpful resources to give you a place to start. You'll find them in the appendix along with lists of bookstores, libraries, media, bloggers, and more. Read on!

Anamcara Press LLC

A Recipe to Market Your Book

Appendix

TAKE YOUR BOOK TO THE STARS, AND HAVE FUN ON THE RIDE!

HTTPS://ANAMCARA-PRESS.COM/

What's Inside This Appendix?

Articles About Book Marketing iii
Bloggers iv
Book Awards v
Book Fairs & Festivals x
Book Reviewers xi
Book Store Lists xvi
Book Store Categories xvii
Letters & Scripts xviii
Libraries xx
Media xxi
Newspaper Reviewers xxii
Promotion Services xxix
Paid Review Services xxx
Speaker's Bureaus xxxi

This appendix contains lists of resources.
Always check details as people and addresses change, including URLs. While we try to keep this appendix up-to-date and work to ensure the links work, we cannot guarantee that all links will take you where you expect to go. We hope we've provided enough detail to enable your search.

MARKET YOUR BOOK!
HTTPS://ANAMCARA-PRESS.COM/

Articles About Book Marketing

Here are some great articles with information about book marketing. Dig in and have some fun!

Articles About Marketing

- An Author's Guide to Creating Successful Book Events:

  https://www.authorsguild.org/member-services/writers-resource-library/authors-guide-to-creating-successful-book-events/

- How to Submit Metadata for a Book on Goodreads:

  https://www.wikihow.com/Submit-Metadata-for-a-Book-on-Goodreads

- How To Use Bookbub to Sell Books:

  https://thewritelife.com/bookbub/?utm_source=The+Write+Life&utm_campaign=d2ff1a5dbb-main_list_11_6_13_11_5_2013&utm_medium=email&utm_term=0_ae07a22b59-d2ff1a5dbb-121024457&mc_cid=d2ff1a5dbb&mc_eid=260f0dc7fc

- Goodreads Author Program:

  https://www.goodreads.com/author/program

- Marketing to Libraries: Basics:

  http://libguides.ala.org/marketing-to-libraries

Online Author Resources

- Free and Paid Book Promotion Services in 2020 by Reedsy:

  https://blog.reedsy.com/book-promotion-services/?utm_campaign=reedsylearning&utm_source=amazon.algorithms&utm_medium=newsletter

- How To Do It Frugally: Alphabetical Listing of Major Review Journals:

  https://www.howtodoitfrugally.com/major_review_journals.htm

- What's a sponsored Review and Why Would I Want One?

  https://citybookreview.com/submission-guidelines/sponsored-review/

- The Indie Authors Guide to Paid Reviews, PW:

  https://www.publishersweekly.com/pw/by-topic/authors/pw-select/article/64718-the-indie-author-s-guide-to-paid-reviews.html

- Optimize Your BISAC Codes in 8 Steps:

  https://www.inscribedigital.com/2015/10/07/metadata-mindset-optimize-your-bisac-codes-in-8-easy-steps/

MARKET YOUR BOOK!
HTTPS://ANAMCARA-PRESS.COM/

Bloggers

Blogger List

You can contact bloggers about book reviews & guest blogging:

- Atlantic Way Review - a comprehensive list of book promotion sites
- Book Review Directory – a comprehensive, alphabetical listing of book blogs, organized by genre.
- The Book Blogger List – a database of book bloggers organized by genre of interest.
- Goodreads - offers writers the chance to exchange reviews with their peers.
- The Indie View – huge listing of Indie reviewers.
- Kate Tilton's Book Bloggers – a smaller listing of book bloggers that provide reviews.
- Self-Publishing Review - For a fee, authors can receive animpartial, editorial book review. The site also ofers paid editing services.
- Story Cartel – all books on Story Cartel are free in exchange for honest book reviews.
- YA Book Blog Directory – a listing of young adult book review blogs.

Blogs & Podcasts

Bloggers want their job of interviewing you to go smoothly & be easy, (the same is true for interviewers from any other media.) Help them by:

- Research the blogger enough to know what their blog highlights. Make sure it's the right blog for your book.
- Send blogger a short article on the topic you propose to discuss on their blog—fit the article to the blog.
- Don't send a book chapter, although your book's chapters can become blog posts on your website.
- Don't expect to present a chapter, instead make your article about the topic of your book more generally.
- Do expect to present a short excerpt from your book & try to work that into your article.
- Do send your media kit & your book electronically
- Readers love to put quotes on Twitter and Facebook. so give them little bites of wisdom from your book that they can easily share with their friends.

MARKET YOUR BOOK!
HTTPS://ANAMCARA-PRESS.COM/

Book Awards

Send book with media kit & letter to relevant awards after publication.

Things change! Double-check deadline, contact, address, and requirements before sending your book for an award.

DEADLINE	AWARD	COST	INSTRUCTIONS
January 31	Foreword Foreword INDIES Book of the Year Awards 425 Boardman Ave Traverse City MI 49684 Web: https://publishers.forewordreviews.com/awards/#service-indiefab-awards	Cost to Enter: $99	The IndieFab Awards recognize the best in indie book publishing, and has been doing so for fifteen years. Our prestigious awards honor great indie books with over 248 winners in 62 categories annually. A panel of over 100 librarians and booksellers determine the winners of these prestigious awards.
January 31	Book Live Prize (Publishers Weekly)		1/31/20 The entry period for the Nonfiction Contest is now open through January 31, 2020. Click here for information on how to enter. Entry period for the next Ficiton Contest will run from April 1, 2020, through August 31, 2020.
January 15	National Indie Excellence Awards - fiction	$99 per entry, and $79 for additional categories.	Register your book for the Foreword INDIES

MARKET YOUR BOOK!
HTTPS://ANAMCARA-PRESS.COM/

January 1	Eric Hoffer Book Award - all categories	$62	Two-year sliding window for regular category entry. Since our registration desk remains open all year long, January 21 is the official registration cutoff date for all books either published or copyrighted in the prior two years. A grand prize of $2,500 is awarded annually. In addition, Eric Hoffer Award honors include various prizes within eighteen all-inclusive categories, separate press distinctions, the Montaigne Medal, the da Vinci Eye, and the First Horizon Award.
January 31	William Saroyan International Prize for Writing - new books		
February 1	Binghamton University John Gardner Fiction Book Award Guidelines - poetry	$0	$1,000 Award for a book of poems written in English, 48 pages or more in length, selected by our judges as the strongest collection of poems published in 2018. send application to Two copies of each book should be sent to: Maria Mazziotti Gillan, Director Creative Writing Program Binghamton University Department of English, General Literature, and Rhetoric Library North Room 1149 Vestal Parkway East P.O.Box 6000 Binghamton, NY13902-6000
January 1 - February 28	Assoc for Writers and Writing Programs - Fiction	$0	Novel: at least 60,000 words.
Nominations for books published in 2019 will be accepted beginning Friday, January 11, 2020 - March 17	High Plains Book Award - life on the high plains (Kansas)	$45 each category	Reader copies should be shipped to: Dee Ann Redman, High Plains Book Awards, Billings Public Library, 510 N 28th St, Billings, MT 59101

MARKET YOUR BOOK!
HTTPS://ANAMCARA-PRESS.COM/

May 17 for Oct Award	National Book Awards - fiction	Cost to Enter: $135	Submissions for the National Book Awards open each March. The book must have been published by a U.S. publisher between December 1 of the previous year and November 30 of the current year. The Foundation sends the official guidelines and submission forms to publishers in its database. Mail one copy of each entered book to the Foundation and each of the five judges in the appropriate category by July1.
8 March - June 14	Man Booker Prize for fiction	$0	Marion Fraser Four Culture 20 St Thomas Street London SE1 9BF marion.fraser@fourcommunications.com Tel: 020 3697 4256
Spring	Aspen Words		http://www.aspenwords.org/, nonprofit literary organization
April 1	Readers' Favorite	$99	Published and unpublished books, eBooks, audiobooks, comic books, poetry books +
June	Sarton Women's Book Award	$90 - $110	Works by women authors Awards are presented annually in four categories. Lesbian entries are welcome in all categories.
January - September	Authors' Zone Awards - all categories		http://www.theauthorszone.com/
September	Firecracker Awards		Submissions to the 2021 Firecracker Awards will be accepted from September 16 to November 15, 2020.
September	The 16th Annual "Best Book" Awards Sponsored by American Book Fest	$69 before 1/31/20	Accepts submissions for books published in 2017 and- 2019 for the 2020 award.
Dec 31, 2020 (for the 2021 Fiction award)	2018 Hefner Heitz Kansas Book Award in Literary Nonfiction (2019 in Poetry, 2020 in Fiction) - non fiction	$0	Books must have an original publication date within three calendar years immediately preceding the year of the competition deadline. For example, to be eligible for the 2020 Novel deadline, the nominee's book must have a publication date of 2017 - 2019 for the 2021 award.

September 1 through December 31	Anisfield-Wolf Book Awards Fiction and nonfiction		Recently published book that "contributes to our understanding of racism and our appreciation of the rich diversity of human cultures" $10,000 cash as well media and publicity opportunities. Submissions must be published in the prior year (so books published in 2019 are eligible for the 2020 award).
June 1 - Aug 15	PEN/Hemingway Award for Debut Fiction	$85*	Complete the on-line submission form THEN mail one copy : PEN/Hemingway Award PEN America 588 Broadway, Suite 303 New York, NY 10012 Once the submitted book is received and reviewed for eligibility by PEN, you will be contacted by awards@pen.org before the end of the year and asked to ship one copy of the book to each of our awards judges.
December	W.Y. Boyd Literary Award for Excellence in Military Fiction	$0	Complete the on-line application and send seven (7) copies of the book to ALA Awards Program Governance Office 50 East Huron Street Chicago, IL 60611 $5,000 to the best piece of fiction set during a period when the U.S. was at war (war may either be the main plot of the piece or simply provide the setting).
December	The Scott O'dell Award - historical fiction	$0	A book intended for children or young people, it must be set in the New World (Canada, Central or South America, or the United States), it must be published by a publisher in the United States, and it must be written in English by a citizen of the United States.
November - January 30th	The Little Rebels Children's Book Award - children's		The Little Rebels Award recognizes children's fiction (for readers aged 0-12) which promotes social justice or social equality, challenges stereotypes or is informed by anti-discriminatory concerns. published between Jan 1st and Dec 31st.

September 2021	IBPA Ben Franklin Awards		Publishers of print books and audiobooks with a copyright date of 2020 may enter the current competition. There are two deadlines for entry (September 30, 2020 and December 15, 2020).
January	North Texas Book Festival - all categories		Books published up to 18 months prior to the start of the Festival CONSIDERED, priority is given to books published within the Festival year. All authors who are invited to participate will be featured in a panel or solo session; Authors must be prepared to cover their own travel expenses to participate in the Festival in Austin, Texas.
Anytime	Nonfiction Authors Book Award Nonfiction Authors Association, 11230 Gold Express Drive #310-413, Gold River, CA 95670.	$300	Mail 3 copies after paying

Children's Book Awards:
- -Book List & School Library Journal
- -Ippy Awards, http://www.ippyawards.com/
- -International Book Award, http://www.internationalbookawards.com/
- -Niea National Indie Excellence Award, https://www.indieexcellence.com/
- -Nabe Pinnacle Book Achievement Awards, The Library Thing
- -Purple Dragonfly Award, https://www.dragonflybookawards.com/purple-dragonfly

Poetry Awards:
- If the title you're submitting is your first book of poetry, submit it to the Kate Tufts Discovery Award. If you've previously published one or more full-length collections of poetry, please submit your book for the Kingsley Tufts Poetry Award. http://www.cgu.edu/pages/6422.asp
- The Pushcart Prize is an American literary prize by Pushcart Press that honors the best "poetry, short fiction, essays or literary whatnot" published in the small presses over the previous year. Magazine and small book press editors are invited to nominate up to six works they have featured.

MARKET YOUR BOOK!
HTTPS://ANAMCARA-PRESS.COM/

Book Fairs & Festivals

Anamcara Press brings all books we publish to all book events we attend. All authors are invited! You might also want to attend the following book fairs & festivals:

1. ALA American Library Association annual conference; Chicago, Illinois. Held in June
2. Bologna Children's Book Fair, April, Bologna, Italy.
3. BookCon, June, NYC.
4. Book Expo of America Conference: Javits Center, NYC. Held in spring
5. Frankfurt Book Fair Publisher's Rights Corner; Frankfort, Germany. Held in fall
6. High Plains Book Fest: Billings, MT. Held in fall
7. London Book Fair: London, England. Held in spring
8. Montana Book Festival, September, Missoula, Montana.
9. The Printer's Row LitFest: Dearborn, MI; Held in June;
10. Word on the Street: Toronto Book and Magazine Festival, September, Toronto, Ontario.
11. Yall Fest: Charleston Young Adult Book Festival, November, Charleston, South Carolina.
12. Miami Book Fair, November, Miami, Florida.

Book Reviewers

Request book reviews from editorial reviewers by following their guidelines. Send books to reviewers from the following list 3-4 months prior to publication.

When you request a review from an editorial reviewer, they'll expect a cover letter from your publisher and your book's media kit, as well as copies of your print or eBook.

Things change! Double-check date, contact, address, and requirements.

REVIEWER Fiction/Non-fiction:	ADDRESS	DETAIL
American Book Review Fiction/Poetry	American Book Review University of Houston-Victoria 3007 N Ben Wilson Victoria, TX 77901	Submit anytime. If your book is selected for review and the review is published we will notify you. reviews frequently neglected published works of fiction, poetry, and literary and cultural criticism from small, regional, university, ethnic, avant-garde, and women's presses.
ALA http://www.ala.org/acrl/choice/publisherinfo	CHOICE 575 Main St., Suite 300 Middletown, CT 06457-3445 Phone: 860-347-6933	Academic. We review current materials only. only finished copies of books; each title include publication date, distributor information, price, and ISBN. No review will be published without a price in U.S. dollars.
Booklist *	Booklist American Library Association 50 E. Huron St. Chicago, IL 60611	Donna Seaman, Editor, Adult Books Books for Youth (Children's and YA): Sarah Hunter, Editor, Books for Youth Contact editorial assistant Ada Wolin for questions about review status.

MARKET YOUR BOOK!
HTTPS://ANAMCARA-PRESS.COM/

Bookreporter.com Fiction/Non-fiction	The Book Report, 850 Seventh Avenue, Suite 901, New York, NY 10019,	The Book Report Network is comprised of 5 other on-line book review / author feature sites: ReadingGroupGuides.com 20SomethingReads.com Teenreads.com (for teens ages 12-18) Kidsreads.com (for kids ages 6-12) GraphicNovelReporter.com. Typically books are reviewed within 3 months of publication.
Chicago Review of Books	on-line	GUIDELINES; unpublished poetry, fiction, and nonfiction. Our open submissions period will close on June 15, 2020
Chicago Tribune & Algren Lit Award	Books Editor 435 North Michigan Avenue ChicagoIllinois60611	Submissions for the 2020 Nelson Algren Literary Award are open from Nov. 21, 2019, at 10:00 p.m. Central Time to January 31, 2020, at 11:59 p.m. Central. guidelines.
City Book Review	on-line	free within 90 days; paid available too Heidi Komlofske-Rojek 930 Alhambra Boulevard, Suite 240 SacramentoCalifornia95816 reviews@citybookreview.com (855) 741-8810
Colorado Review	9105 Campus Delivery Dept. of English, CSU Fort insColorado80523-9105 creview@colostate.edu	http://coloradoreview.colostate.edu/colorado-review/submit/
Compulsive Reader	online; 1st email: maggieball@compulsivereader.com	http://www.compulsivereader.com/submissions/ Literary fiction and poetry, interviews with authors and musicians. If you would like your book to be featured, please send a brief (1-2 paragraph) synopsis, and if we feel that there's a fit, we will contact u.
Economist	The Economist's Deputy Books Editor Adam Barnes	https://mediadirectory.economist.com/people/adam-barnes-3/

Foreword Magazine	Book Review Editor / Foreword Reviews 425 Boardman Avenue Traverse City Michigan 49684 E-mail: mschingler@forewordreviews.com	Review copy (printed or digital) of the title in question must be received in the Foreword offices a minimum of four (4) months ahead of publication. Submit eBooks by email to eBooks+magazine@forewordreviews.com. 1 or pdf
Indie Reader	IndieReader • PO Box 43121 • Montclair, NJ 07043	$250 for review; $75 to expedite/ 2 copies
KC Star		Mike Fannin Editor and Vice President 816-234-4345; Greg Farmer Managing Editor 816-234-4321
Los Angeles Review of Books	Los Angeles Review of Books 6671 Sunset Blvd., Suite 1521 Los Angeles, CA 90028	https://lareviewofbooks.org/about/contact/#!
LA Times		https://www.latimes.com/la-tm-guidelines-story.html
Lambda	William Johnson P.O. Box 20186 New York New York 10014 wjohnson@lambdaliterary.org	http://www.lambdaliterary.org/contribute/how-to/ 3 to 4 months in advance of publication date. Those publishers (small houses) that cannot supply advance galleys may submit finished books, but these should be sent as early as possible with the words "In lieu of galleys"
Library Journal *	Book Review Editor Library Journal 123 William St., Suite 802 New York, NY 10038	"In lieu of galleys" and the publication date affixed to the cover. We generally avoid reviewing books later than date of publication, though we do make exceptions for reference and heavily illustrated works. no children's
Kirkus * **Fiction/Non-fiction**	Laurie Muchnick, Kirkus Reviews, 65 West 36th St., Suite 700, New York, N.Y. 10018.	4-5 months before publication date. As soon as a book is reviewed—almost always, this will be 2-3 months before its publication date—the publisher is notified of the issue date. we require two copies of the finished book when available. adult hardcover or original trade-paperback fiction, general-audience nonfiction and children's and teen books.

Midwest Book Review Publishes book publicity & marketing list	James A. Cox Editor-in-Chief Midwest Book Review 278 Orchard Drive Oregon, WI 53575 1-608-835-7937 mbr@execpc.com e-mail: mwbookrevw@aol.com	Aims to support small publishers; Two copies of the **published** book. A cover letter. A publicity or press release. an approximate 14 to 16-week "window of opportunity" for a book to be assigned out for review.
Neon Books	E-mail: info@neonmagazine.co.uk	https://www.neonbooks.org.uk/review-guidelines/
NYT	Editor The New York Times Book Review 229 W. 43rd Street New York, New York 10036 Children's books attention Children's Book Editor.	Editor The New York Times Book Review 620 Eighth Avenue, 5th Floor New York, NY 10018 4 mo prior Read more: http://www.trainingauthors.com/the-new-york-times-book-review/#ixzz5eYswua11
Pleiades Book Review	Pleiades Book Review Department of English, Martin 336 University of Central Missouri, Warrensburg 64093	http://www.pleiadesmag.com/submit/ send one copy
http://portlandbookreview.com/submission-guidelines-2/	Portland Book Review 465 NE 181st Ave #266 Portland, OR 97230	We prefer to review books that have been released in the past 12 months. Send two copies
Publisher's Weekly Children's/Fiction/Non-fiction	Publisher's Weekly Children's Book; Editor, Diane Roback, 360 Park Avenue South, New York, NY 10010 Publishers Weekly Nonfiction Reviews [or "Poetry Reviews" or other relevant category] 71 West 23 St. #1608 New York, NY 10010	ePub or PDF files. more than 30MBs, it is likely to time out during upload. In those cases we recommend hosting your file in a service like Dropbox and adding the link to access your file to the "Download URL" field in the GalleyTracker submission form. https://www.publishersweekly.com/pw/corp/submissionguidelines.html Submissions must be sent three 3-4 mo prior to publication.

Rain Taxi Review of Books	Rain Taxi PO Box 3840 Minneapolis, MN 55403	quarterly print publication featuring reviews of literary fiction, poetry, and nonfiction, with an emphasis on works that push the boundaries of language, narrative, and genre.
School Library Journal *	SLJ Book Review, School Library Journal, 123 William St., Suite 802, New York, NY 10038	Two copies three months before the month of publication. Send materials to: SLJ Book Review, School Library Journal, 123 William St., Suite 802, New York, NY 10038 For questions related to book submissions to SLJ, please contact Kiera Parrott; kparrott@mediasourceinc.com
The Literary Review (TLR)	285 Madison Avenue MadisonNew Jersey07940 E-mail: info@theliteraryreview.org	http://www.theliteraryreview.org/submit/ Fall submissions only
University departments	KU/Washburn art department: 864-4042; history, English, Psychology, American Studies departments, Social Work etc.	Ask for a referral for someone who would be interested in reviewing
Vol. 1 Brooklyn	Send all books and music for review to: Vol. 1 Brooklyn C/O Jason Diamond 36 Plaza St. E. Apt. 6A. Brooklyn NY, 11238	https://greenmountainsreview.com/ http://www.vol1brooklyn.com/contact/
Washington Post	The Washington Post Attn: Book World 1301 K Street, NW Washington, D.C. 20071	Zero guidelines
WSJ	newsroom@wsj.com	

* Reviews from *Booklist, Library Journal, Kirkus, Publisher's Weekly*, and *School Library Journal* are highly coveted.

Book Store Lists

Bookstores, giftshops, and libraries require books they shelve to have distributable ISBNs.

(Exception: local bookstores and libraries might shelve a self-published book without a distributable ISBN if you ask!)

Lists of Bookstores

- List of Independent Local Bookstores:
- Indiebound.org https://www.indiebound.org/indie-next-list
- NewPages Guide to Indie Bookstores in Kansas
- The best list of independent Kansas bookstores
- 50 Of The Best Indie Bookstores In America

Local & Regional Bookstores

Cold Calls to Bookstores

Once your book is in Ingram and Baker and Taylor distribution, cold calls to bookstores really work. Here's a sample script:

- Author: Hi, I'm an author! Could you check my ISBN?
- Store: Let me connect you with the right department.
- Author: Hi there, I'm an author! Could you check my ISBN?
- Store: Sure, What is it? (Checks the computer) Okay, I have it.
- Author: Great! Could I ask you to order a few for your store?
- Store: Yes, that's fine.
- Author: Thank you so much!

Book Store Categories

- Accounting
- Adventure
- Advertising
- African American Interests
- Alternative
- Americana, Regional, Native
- Animal Rights, Pets
- Anthropology
- Archaeology
- Architecture/Interior Design
- Art
- Asian Studies
- Astrology, Occult, Mythology
- Astronomy
- Audio Books & CDs
- Automotive
- Aviation, Aeronautics
- Behavioral Sciences
- Biblical Studies, Escatology
- Biography/Autobiography
- Biological Sciences
- Body, Mind, Spirit
- Business/Marketing
- Cancer
- Career Development
- Chemistry/Chemical Engineering
- Child Care & Development
- Children's Books
- Christian Books
- Collection & Credit
- Communications
- Computer Science
- Computers and Software
- Construction
- Cookbooks
- Crafts, Hobbies
- Criminology
- Current Affairs
- Developing Countries
- Disabilities/Physical Challenges
- Drama/Theater
- E-books/Electronic Media
- Earth Sciences
- Economics
- Education
- Employment Resources
- Energy
- Energy Alternatives
- Engineering
- Environment Studies
- Estate Planning
- Ethnicity
- Family Care/Parenting
- Farm Equipment & Tractors
- Fiction
- Film, Video
- Finance
- Financial Investments
- Folklore
- Foreign Countries
- Foreign Language Books
- Fund Raising
- Future Events
- Games, Holiday Gifts
- Gardening/Landscaping
- Gay and Lesbian
- Genealogy
- Geography/Geology
- Government/Lobbying/Politics
- Health/Nutrition/Fitness
- Hispanic Interests
- History
- Housing/Low Income
- How-To
- Human Relations
- Human Interest
- Humor/Satirical Collections
- inspiration
- Journals/Periodicals
- Journalism
- Kids & Money Management
- Language Arts/Linguistics
- Lap Swimming
- Law
- Library/Reference
- Literature/Essays
- Management
- Maritime
- Mathematics
- Medicine/Nursing/Dentistry
- Medicine – Alternative
- Men's Interests
- Metaphysical
- Military
- Music/Dance
- Mysteries
- Nature/Natural History
- New Age
- Nonfiction (General)
- Nostalgia
- Other (Miscellaneous)
- Outdoor Recreation
- Parapsychology
- Performing Arts/Acting School
- Pets, Animal Rights
- Philosophy
- Photography
- Physics
- Planned Giving
- Poetry
- Politics, Government
- Prophecy
- Psychology/Psychiatry
- Psychotherapy
- Public Administration
- Publishing/Book Trade Ref.
- Radio/Television
- Railroad
- Real Estate
- Relationships
- Religion
- Romance/Sexuality
- Science (General)
- Science Fiction/Fantasy/Horror
- Securities
- Self-Help/Self-Improvement
- Senior Citizens
- Social Sciences/Sociology
- Spiritual Fulfillment
- Sports/Athletics
- Statistics
- Suspense/Thrillers
- Swimming
- Technology
- Theology
- Terrorism
- Transportation
- Travel/Dining
- True Crime
- Veterinary Science
- Wine and Spirits
- Women's Interests, Feminist
- World War II/Holocaust
- Young Adults

Letters & Scripts

Request book reviews by asking people to read your book and leave a review on Amazon, Goodreads, or other bookseller's website.

When you request a review from an individual that you know, or are friends with on Facebook or other social media platform, they may be blocked from leaving a review for your book by Amazon. Amazon also has spending requirements for anyone leaving a review for a product. They may still be able to leave a review for you on Goodreads.

If you know other authors in your genre, ask them about cross promotion. Find blogs and websites dedicated to your genre. As you interact, you can request reviews from members. Get active on Goodreads!

SAMPLE MESSAGE:

Subject: Can you do me a favor?

Dear Name of person, Describe your book in 1-2 sentences and ask them if they'd be willing to read your book and give you some feedback about it. Ask if they want to receive a PDF, e-book, or paperback to read and review. Give them a deadline.

FIRST SAMPLE MESSAGE TO READER

Subject: My New Book

Hi [First Name],

I hope you're well! [Add a personal intro sentence here]. Over the past [time period], I've been working on a book called *[title of book]*, about [book description].

The way publishing a book works these days, one of the most valuable things I can do is launch the book with reader reviews on Amazon. That's why I'm writing you. Would you like to receive a free copy of my book? I would be happy to send you either a digital copy or a physical copy — whichever you prefer.

If you can read my book I'd also sincerely appreciate it if you considered leaving an honest review once it launches on [street date]. It's by no means necessary, but would be much appreciated.

If you want a physical copy, just reply with your address and I'll ship it out to you ASAP. If you'd prefer a digital copy, just reply and let me know and I'll email it to you. Thanks so much for your time!

MARKET YOUR BOOK!
HTTPS://ANAMCARA-PRESS.COM/

SECOND MESSAGE:

Subject: [First name], [Book Title] Launches in a Week!

Hi [First name],

I wanted to say thanks for agreeing to read [Book Title]. I can't tell you how much it means to me to get this book out in the world on [Date].

I'm writing you to see if you had any questions or feedback before the book launches. If you are open to leaving a review but are not sure what to say about the book or in a review in general, it's totally fine to just leave your general thoughts.

One last thing: if you decide to leave a review, it's important to mention that you received a review copy of the book.

THIRD MESSAGE:

Subject: It's Launch Day For [*Book Title*]

Hi [First name],

Morning! I wanted to send a quick and easy reminder that [*Book Title*] has launched and is available on Amazon! Thank you again for giving it a look before launch. It means a lot.

If you'd like to leave your thoughts on the book in a review, you can do so here (it would be greatly appreciated):

Click here to leave a review for [*Book Title*]. (Add a few detailed instructions).

Again, I can't tell you how much it means that you've taken the time to help out with the book launch. If there's anything that I can do for you, please don't hesitate to ask.

Set up Amazon Author Central Account Where Readers Leave Reviews For Your Book

- Log in & list books - ADD MORE BOOKS; author page for bio, photo, blog, (add RSS feed ex: http://samspade.com/feed/); Add book description & reviews under book details; link books together

- Add tag this product on your books detail page

- Use Amazon list mania feature to drive traffic

- Participate in an on-line, self-guided amazon interview for authors featured with title at amazon.com

- Write reviews: You can write reviews of other related titles and include your book title as part of your signature on the review.

- Buy X get Y paid placement for grouping high-selling book with new book (Costs)

MARKET YOUR BOOK!
HTTPS://ANAMCARA-PRESS.COM/

Libraries

Bookstores, giftshops, and libraries all require books they buy and shelve to have distributable ISBNs.

(Exception: local bookstores and libraries might shelve a self-published book with out a distributable ISBN if you ask!)

List of libraries state-by-state

- WWW Libraries State-by-State

The Libraries routinely acquire books published by commercial publishers that fit the Library's selection criteria and priorities for selection. A positive review in one or more of the major review journals (such as Library Journal, School Library Journal, Kirkus Reviews, Booklist, and/or Publisher's Weekly) is the best way to bring a title to their attention. They are more likely to consider the addition of a book if it has been reviewed in a major review journal.

Library purchasing guidelines for authors

From the Denver Public Library website

1. Basic bibliographic information about your book (title, author, ISBN, publisher, date of publication, number of pages, price, distributor).
2. A link to your book's website and links to professional reviews or other coverage in the news media (if available).
3. A brief description of your book and its intended audience and information about how or where to buy it.

Media

TV, Radio, Newspapers

List of TV Stations

TV Stations US: Resease Ads/interviews (https://en.wikipedia.org/wiki/Lists_of_television_stations_in_the_United_States)

TV Local/Regional with guest oriented segments: Resease Ads/interviews (list: https://en.wikipedia.org/wiki/List_of_television_stations_in_Kansas)

- ID: "FOX 4" City: Kansas City, MO
- 5 KCTV CBS City: Kansas City, MO
- 6 (15) KMOS PBS City: Sedalia, MO
- 9 (29) KMBC ABC City: Kansas City, MO
- 19 KCPT PBS City: Kansas City, MO
- 29 (31) KCWE The CW ID: "kcwe 29" City: Kansas City, MO
- 38 KMCI Independent ID: "38 The Spot" City: Lawrence, KS
- 41 (42) KSHB NBC ID: "Action News" City: Kansas City, MO
- 50 KPXE City: Kansas City, MO
- 62 KSMO My Network TV ID: "MY KSMO TV" City: Kansas City, MO

Book focused programs:

- BOOKNOTES https://www.c-span.org/series/?booknotes

List of Radio stations

- https://en.wikipedia.org/wiki/Lists_of_radio_stations_in_the_United_States

List of Newspapers US

- https://en.wikipedia.org/wiki/List_of_newspapers_in_the_United_States

List of Newspapers KS

- KANSAS! MAGAZINE
- LJW 832-7297
- KU paper 785-766-1491
- Pitch 816-218-6735
- KC Star 816-234-4390

List of NPR Stations

- NPR stations: lists only stations. You'll have to separately google phone number.
- NPR book program: https://www.npr.org/books/

Newspaper Reviewers

Send book to newspapers with book review columns.
Things change! Double-check date/contact/address.

Boston Globe, 135 Morrissey Boulevard, P.O. Box 2378, Boston, MA 02125; 617-929-2000. Web: http://www.bostonglobe.com. Reporters and editors: http://www.bostonglobe.com/tools/help/stafflist.

Paul Nakishima, Books Editor; 617-929-2905. Email: makishima@globe.com. Web: http://www.bostonglobe.com/arts/books.>

Amy Sullivan, Globe Correspondent, interviews authors. Twitter: http://twitter.com/globebiblio. Email: amysutherland@mac.com.

Kate Tuttle, Globe Correspondent, writes The Story Behind the Book and reviews books. Email: kate.tuttle@gmail.com.

Nicole Lamy, the previous book editor, still reviews books for the Globe in the Short Stack column. This email may still be valid: nlamy@globe.com.

Buffalo News, Jeff Simon, Sunday Arts & Books Editor, One News Plaza, P.O. Box 100, Buffalo, NY 14240; 800-777-8680; Fax: 716-856-5150. Email: jsimon@buffnews.com. Web: http://www.buffalonews.com. Features editors: http://www.buffalonews.com/section/help05/#Features.

Charlotte Observer, Dawyne Powell Reading Life Editor, 600 S. Tryon Street, Charlotte NC 28202; 704-358-5024; Fax: 704-358-5036. Email: pkelley@charlotteobserver.com. Pam: 704-358-5271. Web: http://www.charlotteobserver.com or http://www.charlotte.com/mld/charlotte. Staff listings: http://www.charlotteobserver.com/staff.

Contra Costa Times, Sue Gilmore, Book Editor, Bookends, 175 Lennon Lane #100, Walnut Creek CA 94598; 925-977-8482; main phone: 925-935-2525. Email: sgilmore@bayareanewsgroup.com. Web: http://www.contracosta times.com and http://www.mercurynews. com/books. They have just reinstated their book review section in print. Contact list: http://www.contracostatimes.com/contact-us.

Dallas Morning News, Chris Vognar, Culture Editor, Books, P O Box 655237, Dallas TX 75265; 214-977-8594. Email: mmerschel@dallasnews.com. Web: http://www.dallasnews.com/arts/books. Main phone number: 214-977-8222; Fax: 214-977-8838. Lifestyle editors: http://www.dallasnews.com/connectwithus/newsroom_lifestyles.html. Twitter: http://twitter.com/mmerschel.

The Denver Post, Ray Rinaldi, Books Editor, 101 W Colfax Avenue #600, Denver CO 80202; 303-820-1624;Fax: 303-820-1679. Email: Rrinaldi@denverpost.com. Web: http://www.denverpost.com. Editors: http://www.denverpost.com/contactus.

Detroit Free Press, Steve Byrne, Entertainment Editor, 615 West Lafayette Street, Detroit MI 48231; 313-222-5977; Fax: 313-223-4726. Email: spbyrne@freepress.com. Web: http://www.freep.com. Main number: 313-222-6400. Editors: http://www.freep.com/apps/pbcs.dll/article?AID= 200551101001.

Houston Chronicle, Maggie Galehouse, Book Editor, 801 Texas Street (77002-2904), P.O. Box 4260, Houston, TX 77210; 713-362-7171. Email: maggie.galehouse@chron.com. Web: http://www.chron.com.

Indianapolis Star, Jennifer Morlan, Life Editor, 130 S Meridian Street, Indianapolis IN 46225; 317-444-6921. Email: jennifer.morlan@indystar.com. Web: http://www.indystar.com. For a list of reporters, see http://static.indystar.com/en/follow.

International Herald Tribune, 6 bis, rue des Graviers, 92521 Neuilly Cedex, France; (33-1) 41 43 93 22; Fax: (33-1) 41 43 93 32. General email: iht@iht.com. Web: http://www.iht.com. A daily international English-language newspaper owned by the New York Times. Book reviews are taken from the New York Times.

Kansas City Star, Steve Paul, Arts Editor, 1729 Grand Boulevard, Kansas City MO 64108-1413; 816-234-4141; Fax: 816-234-4926. Email: paul@kcstar.com. Web: http://www.kansascity.com. Editorial contacts: http://www.kansascity.com/contact_us. Short book reviews, primarily from other sources.

Los Angeles Times Book Review, 202 West 1st Street, Los Angeles CA 90012; 213-237-7778; Fax: 213-237-5916. Main #s: 213-237-5000; Fax: 213-237-7679. Email: book.review@latimes.com. Web: http://www.latimes.com/ book. Editorial staff: http://www.latimes.com/about/mediagroup/la-mediacenter-editorial_staff,0,3058915.htmlstory. Jacket Copy book blog: http://latimesblogs.latimes.com/jacketcopy. Send email first with as much information as possible to book.review@latimes.com – no attachments.

Miami Herald, Connie Ogle, Book Editor, One Herald Plaza, Miami, FL 33132-1693; 305-376-3649; Fax: 305-376-8950. Email: cogle@miamiherald.com. Web: http://www.herald.com.

Milwaukee Journal Sentinel, 333 W. State Street, P.O. Box 371, Milwaukee, WI 53201; 414-224-2181; General: 414-224-2000. Web: http://www.jsonline.com. Here's what their old book editor once wrote about self-help books: "I would never have bothered with them had it not been for a perverse idea to poke fun at them." This is a common opinion among newspaper book reviewers.

Minneapolis Star Tribune, Laurie Hertzel, Books Editor, 425 Portland Avenue South, Minneapolis, MN 55488; 612-673-4380; Fax: 612-673-7568. Email: hertzel@startribune.com. Web: http://www.startribune.com. General news: 612-673-4414.

Nashville Tennessean, 1100 Broadway, Nashville TN 37203; 615-259-8228; Fax: 615-259-8057. Web: http://www.tennessean.com. Updated 2/17.
New York Post, 1211 Avenue of the Americas, New York, NY 10036; 212-930-8000; Fax: 212-930-8542. Web: http://www.nypost.com.

New York Times Book Review, 620 Eighth Avenue, New York, NY 10018-1405; 212-556-1234 or 212-556-3652; Fax: 212-556-3690. Web: http://www.nytimes.com/books. You can send email to most reporters and critics via the website.

Newark Star-Ledger, Jacqueline Cutler, 1 Star-Ledger Plaza, Newark, NJ 07102; 973-392-4040. Web: http://www.starledger.com. Newsroom contacts: http://www.starledger.com/editorial/News.asp.

Newsday, 235 Pinelawn Road, Melville NY 11747-4250. Web: http://www.newsday.com. Arts & Entertainment Editor, 2 Park Avenue, 8th Floor, New York NY 10016-5695; 212-251-6622; Fax: 212-696-0590. Features/Entertainment (Part 2): 631-843-2950; Fax: 631-843-2065. Option: 631-843-4659.

The Oregonian, Jeff Baker, Book Editor, 1320 S.W. Broadway, Portland OR 97201-9911; 503-221-8165; 877-238-8221, ext. 8165; Fax: 503-294- 5172. Email: jbaker@oregonian.com. Web: http://www.oregonlive.com. Editors: http://biz.oregonian.com/newsRoster.

Philadelphia Inquirer, John Timpane, Books Editor, 801 Market Street #301, Philadelphia PA 19107; 215-854-2401. Email: jt@phillynews.com. Web: http://www.philly.com.

Pittsburgh Post-Gazette, Tony Norman, Book Review Editor, 34 Boulevard of the Allies (15222), P O Box 566, Pittsburgh PA 15230; 412-263-1601; Tony: 412-263-1631; Fax: 412-391-8452. Email: tnorman@post-gazette.com. Web: http://www.post-gazette.com. Twitter: http://www.twitter.com/tonynormanpg.

San Diego Union-Tribune, Robert Krigr, Books Editor, P.O. Box 120191, San Diego, CA 92112-0191; 619-293-1321; 800-244-6397; Fax: 619-293-2436. Email: books@uniontrib.com. Web: http://www.uniontrib.com. Also web: http://www.signonsandiego.com. Pincus's blog: Creative Reading.

San Francisco Chronicle, Barbara Love, Book Editor, 901 Mission Street, San Francisco, CA 94103; 415-777-6258; Fax: 415-957-8737. Email: jmcmurtrie@sfchronicle.com. Web: http://www.sfgate.com. Main phone number: 415-777-1111. Chronicle staff: http://www.sfgate.com/chronicle/info/e-mail.

Seattle Times, 1000 Denny Way, Seattle WA 98109; P O Box 70, Seattle WA 98111; 206-464-2496; Fax: 206-464-2261. Web: http://www.seattletimes.com. Reviews few independent presses outside region. Editorial staff listing: http://seattletimes.com/flatpages/services/newsroomstaff.html.

Tampa Bay Times, Colette Bancroft, Book Editor, 490 First Avenue S (33701), P.O. Box 1121, Saint Petersburg FL 33731; 727-893-8435; 800-333-7505. Email: cbancroft@tampabay.com. Web: http://www.tampabay.com. Contact page: http://www.tampabay.com/company/contact-us.

Tampa Tribune, The News Center, 202 S. Parker Street (33606-2395), P.O. Box 191, Tampa, FL 33601-0191; General: 813-259-7711; Newsroom: 813-259-7600. Web: http://www.tampatrib.com. No book news or reviews.

Toronto Star, One Yonge Street, Toronto, Ontario M5E 1E6 Canada. Web: http://www.thestar.com. Editorial contact: http://www.thestar.com/about/contactus.html#editorial.

Deborah Dundass, Columnist, The Reader. Features Canadian fiction and non-fiction. 416-869-4249. Email: jhunter@thestar.ca. Twitter: http://www.twitter.com/sjenniferhunter (but not active).

Deirdre Baker, Columnist, Small Print. Mini-reviews of books for tots to teens, every other week.>

USA Today, 7950 Jones Branch Drive, McLean VA 22108-0605; 703-854-3400; Fax: 703-854-2053 and 703-854-2049. Email: editor@usatoday.com. Web: http://www.usatoday.com. New York bureau: 535 Madison Avenue, 20th Floor, New York NY 10022. Want to email specific reporters at USA Today? For those that have email addresses, the following formula works most of the time: first-initial-last-name@usatoday.com.

Julia Thompson, Book Editor (based in New York City). Email: jmcclurg@usatoday.com. Twitter: https://twitter.com/jocelynmcclurg

Voice Literary Supplement, Village Voice, 36 Cooper Square, New York NY 10003-4846; 212-475-3300; Fax: 212-475-8944. Email: http://villagevoice.com/feedback/submitSuccess/email. Web: http://www.villagevoice.com. Staff listing: http://www.villagevoice.com/about/staff.

Wall Street Journal, 1211 Avenue of the Americas, New York NY 10036; 212-416-2000. Web: http://www.wsj.com. Christopher Carduff, Books Editor; Sam Sacks, Columnist, Fiction Chronicle; Tom Nolan, Columnist, Mysteries; Tom Shippey, Columnist, Science Fiction
Meghan Cox Gurdon, Columnist, Children's Books

Washington Post, 1150 15th Street N.W., Washington, DC 20071; 202-334-6000; Fax: 202-334-7502. Web: http://www.washingtonpost.com. Editor info: http://projects.washingtonpost.com/staff/email. You can email staff members via that web page. The Post also provides a guide to all the DC area bookstores.

Ron Charles, Fiction Editor. Reports to the Style section. Email: charlesr@washpost.com. Twitter: http://www.twitter.com/roncharles. He also writes and produces his own video blog of book reviews.

Elizabeth Ward, Children's Books. Email: warde@washpost.com. She reviews many children's books. She also works at the copy desk for foreign stories.

Promotion Services

Anamcara Press provides the following marketing services to the authors under our umbrella. We also offer book cover and interior layout design, as well as marketing assistance to independent authors. For comparison, our services include:

- Metadata development & placement
- Book & author branding, including business cards & flyers
- Book media kit/press release
- Print & on-line book release ads & promotional materials
- Assisting authors with creating book release events*
- Assisting authors with sending book for reviews & awards*
- Providing authors with comprehensive marketing guidance (including this book)*

*Starred services are available to Anamcara Press published authors only.

Prior to hosting an event or stocking your book, most bookstores and libraries require authors to have a "platform." A platform, like a portfolio except on-line, includes a website & blog, a landing page for the book directing people to where the book can be purchased, and social media engagement (such as Facebook). Because of this requirement, Anamcara Press also provides the following marketing services for our authors and recommends them to all authors:

- Create/update author website
- Create book landing page
- Social media set up & marketing

MARKET YOUR BOOK!
HTTPS://ANAMCARA-PRESS.COM/

There are many organizations who can assist you with on-line book publicity, developing an author website, and helping to build an author platform. As you'll see from the example on page 29, *The cost of Publicity,* marketing can be very expensive. Review carefully before investing in book marketing to ensure your efforts are not redundant, the charges are competitive, and the service is needed. *Beware of scams!*

Book Marketing Resources
Here are some book marketing organizations who charge for their services.

AUTHOR MARKETING CLUB at https://authormarketingclub.com/members/home/

AUTHOR MARKETING EXPERTS at https://www.amarketingexpert.com/
Penny Sansevieri
10601-G Tierrasanta Blvd. Ste 458
San Diego, CA 92124
(866) 713-2318
info@amarketingexpert.com

CITY BOOK REVIEW at https://citybookreview.com/
3201 Norris Avenue
Sacramento, CA 95821
(855) 741-8810
info@citybookreview.com
FSB ASSOCIATES at https://fsbassociates.com/services.

MINDBUCK MEDIA BOOK PUBLICITY
Jess@MindBuckMedia.com
503.998.8770

(This is not an endorsement of these services. Buyer beware.)

The Cost of Publicity
Example from unnamed service 2018:

	Budget Monthly 2-12 mons $175/month	Internet only 3 mons $1,495	Debut author 4 mons $1,995	Basic 6 mons $2,995	Premium 12 mons $4,995
Start up & promo fees				√	√
Internet presence evaluation		√	√		√
Social media set up assistance			√	√	√
Social media announcements	√	√	√	√	√
Author blurbs sought			√		√
Prepublication reviews sought			√		√
Distribution of review copies			√	√	√
Content evaluation of website		√	√		√
Development of 12 month campaign					√
Scheduling store and library appearances *	√			√	√
Scheduling speaking engagements				√	√
Press release publicity for upcoming events	√		√	√	√
Radio and television interviews *	√			√	√
Blog tours			√	√	√
Placement of blog or print articles	√	√	√	√	√
Submissions for awards				√	√
Assisting author to develop expert status					√

* the number of events depends upon the plan

Prepublication representation, 3 months – $1,495.00 This package is designed to assist authors who've decided to self-publish and need assistance with the process. It includes but isn't limited to:

- Cover art design if needed *
- Formatting if needed *
  FB cover photo, ad design if needed*
- Pricing strategy
- Solicitation of cover blurbs
- Assistance with writing book description and author bio
- Development of basic promo pages
- Evaluation of content for website, Facebook, Goodreads, Amazon, etc.
- Developing an author brand
- Press release for launch
- Assistance with ARC development and distribution
- Seeking advance reviews
- Assistance with planning and scheduling a book launch if desired
- Radio interview for publication week

*additional charges will apply

MARKET YOUR BOOK!
HTTPS://ANAMCARA-PRESS.COM/

Paid Review Services
Companies that charge to review to your book

Here is a list of paid review sites that offer an opportunity for honest reviews for your eBook. You aren't purchasing reviews per se, instead, these sites play matchmaker between authors and prospective reviewers—matching your book with interested, unbiased reviewers who request a review copy of your book based on the cover, blurb, and genre. The following list of reviewers charge for their services, but do guarantee reviews (although not necessarily good ones):

- NetGalley: https://www.youtube.com/watch?v=ZE5OJ5LY67U
- City Book Review (https://citybookreview.com/)
- Hidden Gems (https://www.hiddengemsbooks.com/)
- KO's Stuffed Shelf (https://stuffedshelf.com/)
- Library Thing (https://www.librarything.com/)
- New Apple Book Reviews
- Vine Reviews (https://www.amazon.com/gp/vine/help). Vine Reviews accepts up to 30 reviews for your Amazon book page. The author may ***not*** contact reviewers, unlike NetGalley which has no limit and encourages authors to communicate with reviewers.

Speaker's Bureaus

You are an expert!

Completing your book makes you an expert—if nothing more than at completing a writing project. People may benefit from your expertise, and you can benefit from spreading your knowledge. Standing in front of an audience isn't for everyone, but it is a great way to get new readers for your book!

Speakers Burearus
Here are some to contact:

- National Speakers Bureau: https://nationalspeakers.com/
- Top Speakers Bureau: https://keynotespeakers.info/bureau/
- https://speakerexchangeagency.com/
- https://www.humanitieskansas.org/grants-programs/speakers-bureau
- https://www.speakernow.com/topics/kansas-speakers/
- http://www.kansascityspeakersbureau.com/about-us.htm
- http://alexanderspeakersbureau.com/planTips/KansasCitySpeakers

Authors are Awesome!
Thank you for being an author!

Our world needs interpretation today more than ever. As an author you join a group of highly-valued interpreters of reality. Whether you write fiction or non-fiction, your vision may change the vision of many others!

At Amamcara Press we appreciate all of the hard work and time that goes into writing your book(s). We value the expertise you've gleaned—up to and in the process of writing—and want to help you showcase your book and knowledge. All of the steps provided in this marketing guide are meant to help you get and stay excited about the marketing process. The baby is born; let's introduce her to the world!

We hope you have enjoyed your copy of *A Recipe to Market Your Book*. Please leave a review for Carroll on your favorite booksellers website!
Visit: Anamcara Press (https://anamcara-press.com/

www.ingramcontent.com/pod-product-compliance
Lightning Source LLC
Chambersburg PA
CBHW081801100526
44592CB00015B/2514